NEFERTITI *and* CLEOPATRA

Frontispiece. Tutankhamen's golden throne. *Cairo Egyptian Museum*

NEFERTITI
AND
CLEOPATRA

Queen-Monarchs of Ancient Egypt

JULIA SAMSON

INTRODUCTION BY PROFESSOR H. S. SMITH

The Rubicon Press

The Rubicon Press
57 Cornwall Gardens
London SW7 4BE

First published 1985
Reprinted 1987
Revised 1990
Reprinted 1997

British Library Cataloguing in Publication Data

Samson, Julia
Nefertiti and Cleopatra : Queen-Monarchs of
Ancient Egypt. - New ed.
1. Egypt. Nefertiti, Queen of Egypt 2. Egypt, Cleopatra VII,
Queen of Egypt
I. Title
932.01092

ISBN 0-948695-18-8

Designed and typeset by The Rubicon Press

Printed and bound in Great Britain by Biddles Limited of Guildford
and King's Lynn

Contents

List of Illustrations

vi

DEDICATION

To my dear parents
With loving and happy memories

Acknowledgements

My thanks initially must go to the many Egyptologists and historians who have worked and written over the past years. In this country, Amelia Edwards was the corner-stone in the development of Egyptology. An intrepid traveller, she wrote the best-seller *A Thousand Miles up the Nile* as early as 1877, and when she died in 1891 she bequeathed not only her Egyptological library to University College London, but founded a Chair there, for a Professor of Egyptian Archaeology. She could not have found a greater spearhead for this study than Flinders Petrie, as he then was, who later became the first Professor of Egyptology in this country, and was the genius behind his Collection that has made the present Museum a mine of information. To Professor H. S. Smith, fifth in line of eminent 'Edwards' Professors at University College since Petrie, and a constant stimulus behind the publication of objects in the Museum, my thanks are great indeed, especially for his helpful reading of this book and his re-reading of the original hieroglyphic text of Akhenaten's Poem to the Aten. Today no mention can be made of the Museum without acknowledging the work of its curator, Mrs. Barbara Adams, and I would like to express my personal thanks to her, for her unselfish help so readily given, despite the endless calls on her time made by Museum matters.

Part I of this book is based entirely on the actual finds from Amarna and the publications of all the remains there, and at Luxor. Sir William Matthew Flinders Petrie was the first to excavate there in 1891, and his publication *Tell el Amarna* (reprinted by Aris & Phillips, 1974) is a classic. My thanks also go to all the excavators who have followed him at Amarna, for their work and its publication, mostly by the Egypt Exploration Society, and particularly as follows: J. Pendlebury, *City of Akhenaten* III (but also volumes I (for Leonard Woolley) and II; N. de Garis Davies, six volumes of *The Rock Tombs of El Amarna; The Tomb of the Vizier Ramose;* and *The Mural Paintings of El Amarna* with his wife Nina, Professor Glanville and others, and my ever helpful colleague Geoffrey Martin, for the first volume of *The Royal Tomb of El-'Amarna,* (with volume II in preparation); for the latest finds at Karnak, *The*

Akhenaten Temple Project by D. Redford, J. Gohary, R. Smith and others, (Aris & Phillips, 1974) is basic, and D. Redford, *Akhenaten* (Princeton University Press). The German excavators of the site early this century have never fully published their work, but the illustrated book on the statue head of Nefertiti in Berlin published by the Egyptian Museum, Charlottenburg, West Berlin, is a work of art. Some of the many articles on Amarna history in specialist journals are included in the Reading List. Those of John R. Harris are paramount, as he was the first to define the evidence of Nefertiti's regality. No thanks to specialists can be complete without reference to The Rubicon Press. I offer my warmest gratitude to Anthea Page, an Egyptologist herself, and Juanita Homan, with her expertise in book design, for their untiring care and attention to the publication of this book.

For Part II, the original sources have not been fully given, as so much historical material with references is now available to readers in the Penguin Classics and Penguin Shakespeare Library, but my gratitude is great. Other invaluable modern sources are *Cleopatra*, M. Grant (Panther Books), and *Ancient History Atlas* and *From Alexander to Cleopatra*, both M. Grant (Weidenfeld & Nicolson).

The help of many friends has been a constant encouragement. To Dame Albertine Winner, who called herself my 'medical editor' but the light of whose probing mind on the Amarna text has not been limited by her profession, my thanks are great indeed. I am also grateful to Miss Ann Petrie, Miss Elspeth Mackie, M.B.E., and to Ernst Albert, O.B.E., for their candid and useful criticisms. The particular help of Miss Alison King, O.B.E. sprang from her own experience of converting her specialist knowledge of the Ferry Pilots in the war into a most readable book, and I have often been grateful for her gift of simplification which has helped me over the description of many technical hurdles.

The late Lord Amulree gave me the benefit of his studies of public health in the past, and I thank him for his help in disentangling the scanty evidence we have of this subject at Amarna. I have bowed many times under the merciless questions of Lady E. M. Hooper and Mrs. H.M. Davies to whom I am very grateful for looking at the subject from the 'outside'. Also I thank my neighbour Mrs. Honor Carr for the benefit of her literary insight. To Mrs. John Coker, I can but say that had it had not been for her constant and thoughtful assistance with the time consuming tasks of daily life, for which I am ever grateful, I might never have finished the book. Lastly I thank my two cats for their speechless companionship, and total lack of demand, except at mealtimes when they sat on the manuscript!

Introduction

"The well of the past is very deep", wrote Thomas Mann; and its depths are murky indeed when we try to discern those critical moments that have changed man's history. Yet out of the depths shafts of light seem to pierce the gloom, as if lamps lit by great figures of the past shone eternally upwards from their appointed niches below. Two such luminaries, Nefertiti, consort of the sun-worshipping Pharaoh Akhenaten (1367-1350 B.C.), and Cleopatra VII (51-30 B.C.), the last independent ruler of the Ptolemaic line, form the subject of this book. Both ruled Egypt as female sovereigns at moments deemed critical in history; the names of both appear in the same time-honoured hieroglyphic titulary; but Nefertiti was (to the best of our knowledge) an Egyptian, living at a time when Egypt was the most cultured and one of the most powerful nations on earth, while Cleopatra was a woman of Macedonian race but of Greek culture, living in a post-Hellenic world ever more overshadowed by the power of Rome, and ruling an alien people in a conquered land.

Far apart as they stood in time and culture, however, these two famous women, who have captured the imagination of generations born long after their own eras, invite comparative study by the likeness of their situation. Documented human history is, after all, long or short according to the context in which it is perceived. The 5,000 years since Egypt became a literate, cultured, unified nation-state are impressive indeed when compared with more evanescent civilizations; yet those 250 generations or so represent only the final stage of man's latest evolutionary adventure. Both Nefertiti and Cleopatra belong to our world of ordered, civilized society, far above the muddy bottom of Mann's well, where the human species emerges from the early hominids. Their elegance, their position of power, their remarkable and unusual aims, their failure and tragedy, fascinate by their dramatic quality as much as by their critical historic importance. Yet their study raises fundamental problems concerning the nature and aims of ancient history.

Historians have always seen biography as part of history. Though a wide range of environmental, economic, political, social and religious factors are, with varying degrees of emphasis, considered to contribute to historical causation, no historian denies that on occasion personal character, talent, intellect or actions may have played a role, sometimes a vital role, in past events. Yet for ancient times, our sources are rarely such as to give an inkling of the personality even of the most prominent actors in the drama; or where they purport to do so, there is often good reason to doubt their trustworthiness or impartiality. This leaves the ancient historian in the delicate situation of wishing to introduce into his story the vivid elements of human greatness and error which he knows must have played their part, yet without valid evidence, in the strict sense, for inferring these. This is one reason why ancient history may often make such unsatisfactory reading, why books vary so much in their accounts, why there is so much contest over detail between writers. The wary academic, faced with unreliable sources, or with the problem of inference from insufficient evidence, will tend to stay strictly within the bounds of what he believes can be deduced with a high or at least a quantifiable probability: what is known as 'dry as dust' history. The popular writer will require to bring out the dramatic, the passionate, the human elements in the situation, and will accordingly use source material uncritically or simply invent as he feels fits the situation. Between these two limits, there are many types of compromise, some more satisfactory or justifiable than others; the fundamental problem remains.

Cleopatra has of course attracted constant attention since the Renaissance; her spectacular role in Roman history at just that point where Republic became Empire, her famed liaisons with Julius Caesar and Mark Antony, her suicide, have made her the subject of every species of poetry, drama, myth and history. Nefertiti, however, only emerged from the deeper waters of Egypt's past in the nineteenth century A.D. with the decipherment of the hieroglyphs, the discovery of Akhenaten's capital city of el-'Amarna, and the spectacular excavation of the royal palace by Flinders Petrie in 1892; and perhaps only became firmly embedded in the public consciousness with the publication of the famous Berlin head of the queen after the First World War, and the excavation of the tomb of her direct or near-successor Tutankhamun by Carter and Carnarvon in 1922/3. Even now, Nefertiti is presumably much less of a household word than Cleopatra, though by an ironic accident in the survival of genuine and outstanding portraits, her features are probably the better known. Their comparative study raises in acute form the historical problem alluded to above, for the evidence for understanding the character and personality of each is quite inadequate, but for contrasting reasons.

Evidence concerning Akhenaten and Nefertiti derives almost wholly from sites, monuments, inscriptions and artifacts contemporary with them; for after their death, the form of sun-worship which they instituted as the state-cult was banned, their residence-city of Akhetaten at el-'Amarna was abandoned, their monuments dismantled, destroyed or defaced, and their memory officially expunged from state records. What remains are certain scenes and inscriptions from temples in Egypt and Nubia, those still *in situ* being partly defaced, those dismantled and re-used in the core of buildings undamaged but in need of endless patient piecing together; scenes and inscriptions in the tombs of Akhenaten and Nefertiti's courtiers at el-'Amarna and at Thebes, mostly again defaced; the boundary stelae, badly weathered, of the city of Akhetaten and its extensive but plundered ruins, successively excavated by Petrie, by the German von Sieglin mission and by the Egypt Exploration Society; and a wealth of statues and statuettes, fragments of painting and relief, decorative elements, personal adornments and domestic artifacts of every sort, many of them inscribed and mostly from these excavations. In so far, then, as the evidence is contemporary and, though sometimes defaced, has not been corrupted or distorted by later hands, it may be relied upon. In this work the problems are impartially argued to a conclusion. But apart from the hymns to the sun inscribed in certain nobles' tombs, which do allow us to appreciate something of the character of Akhenaten's and Nefertiti's form of sun-worship and its differences from classical Egyptian beliefs, the majority of the written material is formulaic and repetitive, and little of it gives us information which may be termed 'historical', still less 'biographical'. One salient exception to this is the remarkable archive of diplomatic correspondence between the rulers of the nations and cities of the Near East in the time of Akhenaten and his father Amenophis III, written in cuneiform script in a variety of languages on clay tablets, which were found in the 'Record Office' at el-'Amarna at the end of the 19th century A.D. But this most valuable historical source informs us about conditions in the Levant and Near East, not in Egypt; and, highly significant though one or two detailed references may be, does not throw much direct light upon Nefertiti. Indeed, the types of inscriptional and artifactual evidence which survive provide at best a basis for inference, and are very easily misinterpreted or over-interpreted. They have, no doubt, often been so, even by the great Petrie himself; and there still remains uncertainty and confusion, even in the minds of Amarna scholars, as to the identity of certain royal personages at El-'Amarna and the role that Nefertiti herself played.

On the other hand, classical literature does not lack accounts of Cleopatra, of her life and role in history, and most of these have been long available. None of them, however, is precisely contemporary, and all, whether written in Latin or in Greek, are open to well-founded suspicions that they derive from biased sources, whether these represent Pompey's, Antony's, or Brutus's faction, or the official propaganda of the Augustan empire, or constitute an amalgam of Alexandrian gossip, hearsay and fabrication. None represents Cleopatra's own view, nor even perhaps sources close to her. Source criticism and learned controversy has done much to establish what should be reliable, but, even so, there is still scope for some differences of view. The recovery over the past 90 years of written documents in Greek and demotic Egyptian on papyrus from the rubbish dumps of towns in Egypt and from the cartonnage mummy-cases of sacred animals and humans, has of course provided scholars with much invaluable new historical evidence. But it is fair to say that most of this evidence bears on administrative, economic and commercial history; upon taxation, upon local official practice, upon business, upon farming and domestic affairs. Most of it, too, comes from the country, especially from the Fayum lake-province, not from the capital city of Alexandria. With the personal and political history of Cleopatra, it helps only marginally. Nor has excavation been very helpful, for those parts of the ancient city of Alexandria which modern priorities have allowed archaeologists to work upon have not provided sensational discoveries directly relevant to Cleopatra's history. What has accrued over the years is a steady increase in coin evidence, valuable both historically and in providing new portraits of the queen; and real advances in the study of Ptolemaic portraiture which have led to the discovery, identification and re-identification of portraits of the monarch. There has also been a constant flow of scholarly research, analysis and criticism. Even now however, the contemporary inscriptional and archaeological evidence hardly serves to balance and check the literary accounts.

In this dilemma, it requires a bold author to present an account of modern knowledge of the lives of these two queens to the general interested public, that errs neither on the side of caution nor of speculation. This is particularly the case since no one person can in these days be expert both in Pharaonic and in Hellenistic history, requiring as they do quite different linguistic skills and documentary background. Mrs. Julia Samson, however, has the literary courage, the sense of responsibility to the public, and on the Egyptian side all the scholarly qualifications to essay this task.

Mrs. Samson studied Egyptology under Professor S.R.K. Glanville, Petrie's successor in the Edwards Chair of Egyptology at University College London, in the 1930s. With his encouragement she began to study, catalogue and arrange for exhibition the objects that Petrie had found at el-'Amarna, principally on the site of the Great Palace. The fascinating collection in the Petrie Museum at University College includes some masterpieces, but also a mass of fragmentary material and small objects of great decorative interest and, as it turns out, in some instances of high historical significance. During this work that fine archaeologist John Pendlebury, who lost his life aiding the Cretan partisans during the Second World War, invited her to join the excavations he was directing for the Egypt Exploration Society at el-'Amarna. As a result she contributed a chapter on Petrie's finds to the final report, *City of Akhenaten III*.

War-service claimed her; but after a fruitful career in the Civil Service, she returned as an Honorary Research Assistant to the Petrie Museum in the 1960s to complete her task of cataloguing the 'Amarna collections. She published the first volume of a new series of Petrie Museum catalogues, *Amarna, City of Akhenaten and Nefertiti: Key Pieces in the Petrie Museum* in 1972. She then set herself to analyse thoroughly the detailed material from Petrie's excavations, and found evidence to support Professor J.R. Harris's conclusion that Akhenaten had been succeeded by a woman. Subsequently, she has written numerous articles on 'Amarna history, and revised and expanded her original book to incorporate her new discoveries (1978). She has lived with the fascinating and extraordinary art and culture of the el-'Amarna period from early in her life, and has been in the forefront of the recent researches and scholarly argument which have led to a radical re-appraisal of Nefertiti's history, still not accepted by all.

Mrs. Samson is therefore well-placed to present to the general reading public a full and rounded account of life at the court at el-'Amarna in the 14th century B.C., and the role that Queen Nefertiti played. This is her aim, and in doing so she gathers together and presents the 'Amarna material from the world's great museums, from excavations at el-'Amarna and elsewhere, and the new reliefs found in the interiors of pylons at the temples of Karnak and Luxor; and explains clearly why it is now possible to see Nefertiti as one of the few queens ever to have ruled Egypt as Pharaoh. This, then, is as near as we can as yet get to a biography of an ancient Egyptian monarch; and for the reasons given above, personality and character inevitably remain unfathomed. It is in this respect that the contrast with Queen Cleopatra is interesting, where some of the personal detail as we have derives from mainly historical animosities. Mrs. Samson's research on Cleopatra derives from the work of other scholars. They show clearly how difficult it can be in ancient history to discriminate personal from policy needs, public from private decisions, to judge the interaction of the ruler and the ruled. In this work, set against the unchanging landscape of the Nile valley, the reader sees two of history's most remarkable women; and has opportunity to reflect both on the wonder of what we can know of our past, and upon how much more we should like to know. In the alluvium of the Nile valley and the sands of the Egyptian desert, there still await us discoveries that can revolutionise our knowledge of our past, if we have but the generosity, the resolution and the skill to excavate, analyse and understand the tantalising but fascinating litter of history.

Professor H. S. Smith
Department of Egyptology
University College London

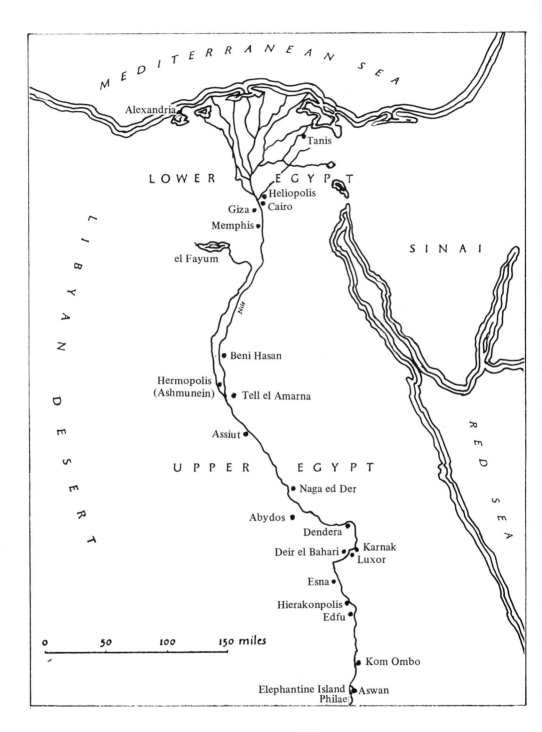

Map of Nile Valley

Prologue: Historic Greatness

Greatness is such a curious and indescribable thing. It sets people above others, but not necessarily people in high positions for many in a modest way of life are great in attributes, although perhaps known only to the few. But both the women in this book were great in stature, in rank and position, known far and wide in their own time and familiar by name in ours. Both were eminent; but very different: Nefertiti, so beautiful that her portrait-head now in the West Berlin Museum holds people transfixed, enthralled as they look at it; Cleopatra, so brilliant that she was a leading figure affecting the history of the world. One thing they had in common was that they were not only great in themselves; they both loved and inspired the greatest men of their time - Nefertiti the famous Pharaoh Akhenaten and Cleopatra both Julius Caesar and Mark Antony. But their worlds, separated by over 1,000 years of history, were as different as that fateful 1,000 years could make them.

Looking way back into Egypt's past, before Akhenaten and Nefertiti, we can see the country was united around 3,000 B.C., under the first king whose name we know, the Pharaoh Narmer (Menes). The early dynasties led into the Old Kingdom and the building of the pyramids, those immense wonders of the world planned by the pharaohs to protect the wealth in their tombs which were, alas, mostly desecrated and ransacked by tomb robbers at or near to the time of the burial.

The history of Egypt waxed and waned. After the Old Kingdom came a period of recession. Then with the advent of a line of mighty pharaohs, it flourished again in the Middle Kingdom about 2,000 B.C., which was followed by another low, the Second Intermediate Period. The weakness of the country at this time encouraged foreigners to invade the rich Delta lands, and the 'Shepherd Kings' (the Hyksos) swept in from the Near East. They even captured Memphis the capital of Lower (Northern) Egypt, apparently without a struggle. They introduced some technical advances such as the general use of bronze instead of the frailer copper, and the horse-drawn chariot, which was never to disappear from Egyptian life. But they got no further.

1

Then came a resurgence of the might of Egypt, with strong pharaohs, and a line of 'Great Queens', not ruling ones, but the principal wives and the mothers of the pharaohs. A queen named Teti-Sheri - meaning literally 'little' Teti - but the smallness was in size alone - was married to the Prince of Thebes (Luxor). Her son Tao 'the brave' challenged the northern invaders but was killed in battle. Nothing daunted his eldest son, Teti's grandson Kamose, continued the fight and when he was eventually killed, his younger brother Amosis carried on the battle for the overlordship of Egypt, and carried it on victoriously. And it was Amosis, this young grandson of Teti's, who became virtually the founder of the XVIIIth Dynasty, and indeed of the New Kingdom, the most powerful period in the country's history, in about 1560 B.C.

In this dynasty, pharaohs sent or led expeditions far and wide for the aggrandisement of Egypt. The Queen-Monarch Hatshepsut (Hat-shep-sut) succeeded her husband Tuthmosis II as pharaoh (Nefertiti being the only Egyptian queen to rule *with* her husband) and Hatshepsut manned an expedition to sail to 'Punt' which was somewhere round the Gulf of Aden, perhaps Somaliland, to bring back ivory and ebony, gold and the fragrances of frankincense and myrrh. She also repaired the temples and other buildings that had suffered at the hands of the Hyksos, and built the loveliest of temples at Deir el Bahri across the Nile from Thebes.

Some of her successors sailed across the Mediterranean to the Near East, the countries we now call Syria and the Lebanon, Israel and Jordan; what used to be Persia and is now Iran, and the older 'Mesopotamia' now Iraq, right over to and past the Euphrates river, from which adventures they returned laden with booty, and hunted lions on the way home. But Egypt remained emphatically, unchangeably Egyptian, with its own particular language expressed in the finely cut hieroglyphs of the wall inscriptions, its civilisation, the brilliance of its sculptures and relief carvings and paintings, and its complicated ancient religions - all a part of itself and only itself.

Not until the King, whose throne name was Amenophis IV, which he eventually changed to Akhenaten (Aken-aten), were differences introduced into the Egyptian ways which were so startling in quantity and quality that they have made his reign an era of interest and fascination ever since, quite apart from all the greatness of Egypt that went before it and came after it: and it is in this reign that we meet the renowned Regnant Queen Nefertiti.

When she was the Regnant Queen with the famous Akhenaten in the 1360's B.C., Egypt was powerful, different and distinguished, and politically separated from the rest of the world. The geographical formation of most of the country, consisting of the long-stretching Nile bordered by the narrow fertile fields with the rocks and sands of the valley beside them and the vast deserts beyond, has always meant isolation. But even in the fan-shaped Delta of the river, watered by its different outlets into the Mediterranean, which were more accessible from the sea - even there it was still essentially Egyptian.

Not until the lst century B.C., did invaders make any real impact on Egypt. But when the Greek conqueror Alexander the Great liberated the country from Persian domination in 332 B.C., he founded a new city on the shores of the Delta, and 'Alexandria' became a Hellenistic centre. After Alexander, Egypt's kings were Greek and all but two were the 'Ptolemies' - of whom the famous Cleopatra was the last. By the time she was King of Egypt in 51 B.C., Alexandria was a cosmopolitan centre, a focus of world trade and culture, and the country was caught up with the rest of the world on the inevitable pathway of becoming a province of Rome. Such were the changes in the years that separated Nefertiti from Cleopatra.

PART I

NEFERTITI
A Regal Queen

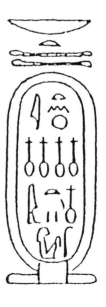

Plate I. Painted limestone head of Nefertiti in West Berlin

I The Creators

In the early years of this century a carved portrait head, unsurpassed in the world of art, was found lying in the sand of central Egypt. Not in the wildest dreams of the German excavators of the time could they have imagined stumbling across such royal beauty, because although unique, the carving was recognisably an ancient Egyptian crowned Queen. But they were excavating hundreds of miles from the capital centres - from Memphis, the administrative capital in the northern Delta of the Nile, and from Thebes (Luxor), the royal stronghold in the south. Little more than a decade or so before this find, Sir Flinders Petrie had partly excavated near this area, at 'Amarna', and he found the remains of a city once greatly decorated, but by then razed to the ground. The Pharaoh of the city was known to have been Akhenaten, shown in the wall-carvings with his crowned Queen, Nefertiti. But this statue-head - a portrait in the round - enables us to see Nefertiti in a way that describes her to us as no words could. It makes it credible that she, with her husband, initiated the building of a new capital city in the desert, far from the very ancient and conventional centres; and that they could change from the age-old worship of hundreds of animal-gods and human-gods to a break-through conception of one beneficent creator of all living things in all the world - the sun - the god Aten - to whom they dedicated the new city now known as Amarna.

This portrait (Pls. I and II) is now in the Egyptian Museum of West Berlin to be wondered at by the thousands who visit it annually. Over and above all Nefertiti's other portraits it is this life-sized painted statue-head of her, that gives us the opportunity to meet her face-to-face, a great artist's gift to us of her personality. The poise of her head on her slim shoulders is caught so perfectly that looking at it one expects her to move: 'it is alive'. The vitality of the woman comes across with such effect that of all portraits it can be called a 'speaking' likeness. Watching people approach it is fascinating in itself. All are held in wonderment, spellbound by its appeal; some immobilised longer than others; some returning not once, but again and again, almost unbelievingly.

Painted in natural colours, Nefertiti's arched eyebrows and eyelashes emphasise the beauty of her large, deep-lidded eyes. The eye is enlivened by a curved inlay of clear, transparent crystal set into the oval. On the inside of this, the iris is painted in the rich dark-brown colour of Nefertiti's eyes, and the outer curve catches the light as it is caught on the curve of a living eye. The eyelid just touches the top of the lovely brown centre and with a slightly downward glance Nefertiti holds the viewer in her serene but responsive look. Although the crystal inlay has fallen from her left eye, her whole face is so captivating that this is somehow easy to overlook. Her small straight nose follows a Grecian line from her brow to her full sensuous lips that lie tranquilly one on the other, lifted slightly by a hovering smile. Her elegant cheek-line is rounded at the feminine chin. Rising straight from her brow, almost soaring over the well-proportioned features in a way few women could carry off, is her unique tall crown, decorated by a coloured band and the cobra worn by 'Great' Queens. The Queen appears to be about thirty years old. Below her slim neck, her shoulders are decorated with a typically wide Amarna necklace made of the coloured beads of flowers, fruit, leaves and petals. And yet, the really compelling quality of the portrait lies in the character displayed in it. The Russian Egyptologist Dr. Perepelkin has written "her infinite charm captured by the ancient artists defies time . . . Her expression gracious, but on the whole commanding and dignified". Professor Anthes of Berlin described her portrait as a "living image . . . complete in itself and drawing on its own fountains of strength". It seems a spiritual power that lies behind the assurance and composure of this face, its intelligence softened by Nefertiti's smile which, like the irresistible charm of her answering look, responds - even today.

Totally unlike the superb naturalism of this portrait-head of Nefertiti from Amarna, are the remains of colossal statues of Akhenaten from the Aten temple they built in Thebes, before they constructed the new capital where the art mellowed. Nothing was left standing of the Theban Aten temple, naturally enough, because although it was in the centre of the stronghold of worship of the god Amen, its walls were covered in painted carved scenes of Akhenaten and Nefertiti worshipping the Aten - and only the Aten. The temple was destroyed by the pharaohs who followed and reverted to the worship of Amen. They had the Aten wall-scenes packed away in the pylon-gateways of their newer temples but fortunately we have some remains of the colossal statues of Akhenaten (Pl. III) which had stood against some thirty, squared pillars of the temple.

Exaggerated as they are, they give us an almost uncanny insight into the mind of the man who broke away from the gods of the traditional religions which had held sway for over 1,000 years before him and which returned to be worshipped for over 1,000 years after his reign. When the statues were first

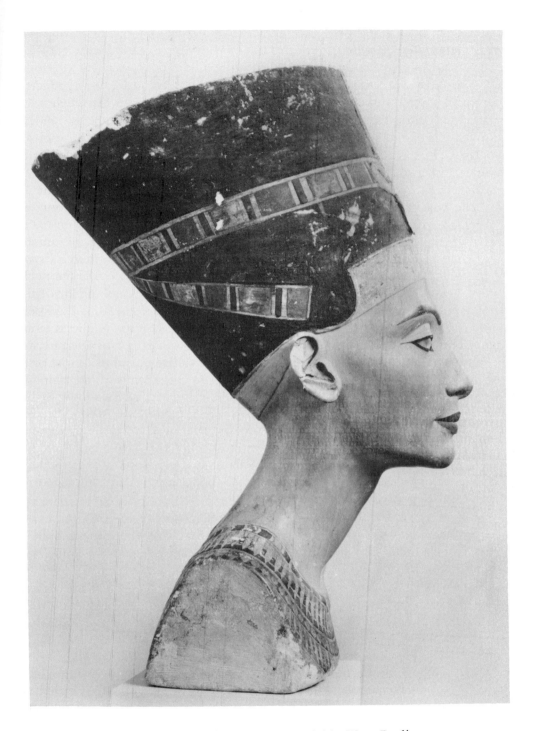

Plate II. Profile head of Nefertiti in West Berlin

found, only some sixty years ago, people were aghast at their unconventional forms. They were shocked and horrified, viewing them as grotesque and they believed they showed Akhenaten was certainly mad. The outcry was as great as that caused by the early works of the French Impressionists, now selling for millions of pounds but at first described as the work of 'savages'. In Thebes, the artists were introducing into their carvings, the element we might now call 'Expressionism' rather than the traditional 'dead likenesses' of the pharaohs of the past. The new art has nowhere been better appreciated than by Jacques Vandier, then of the Louvre, who wrote of Amarna portraits as having *"le mystère d'une vie intérieure intense"*.

The bust shown in Plate III, now in Cairo, seems in a way to express such a brooding mystique. The mood of the large, calm, almond-shaped eyes is repeated in the relaxed half-smiling lips. The exaggeratedly long face is further lengthened by the usual 'pharaoh's beard' strapped on as part of the regalia and by the very *unusual* addition of a curled wig falling each side of it from the Nemes head-dress. The effect was further heightened by tall plumes, now broken, but which once surmounted the head-dress. These accentuated verticals must have given an overwhelming sense of exalted majesty in the standing statue. The squared shoulders with the traditional pose of the crossed arms, and the hands holding the crook and flail - insignia used by pharaohs for centuries past - give a certain balance to the figure. But unlike any other pharaoh, Akhenaten is clasped round the upper arms and wrists by broad bands inscribed with two cartouches (ovals) containing the two names of the Aten - the only god to be thus shown worn by a pharaoh, and the only god to be thus shown resembling a pharaoh in having two names in cartouches. The sun-god Aten was the centre of Akhenaten's and Nefertiti's lives, as developments described and the illustrations later bear out. The concentration portrayed in this face foreshadows the degree of his dedication.

But early, in the Theban period of the reign, we get our first glimpse of Nefertiti from a wall-carving in their old capital, before Amarna was built. It comes from a scene in a Theban tomb and shows her as a willowy young wife behind her husband. (Fig. 1)

Unusually for a pharaoh's 'Great Wife', we have no details of her youth, or where she grew up. But to compensate for that we have more pictures of her in her regal, religious and family life than of any other queen of Egypt. She must always have been beautiful and it is difficult to imagine she was ever a gawky girl; her daughters are certainly never shown as such. Possibly, like Akhenaten's mother, Nefertiti was born in a court family, perhaps daughter of the nobleman Ay. She had sisters at court of whom more is written later. It appears that one married Tutankhamen's successor who was not royal; he was in no way a pharaoh in his own right and possibly he married Nefertiti's sister to strengthen his claim to the throne.

Plate III. Colossus of Akhenaten from the Aten temple at Thebes

Fig. 1. Akhenaten and Nefertiti as a young couple

What we do know about Nefertiti is what her husband thought of her by the way he had her described in the inscriptions in phrases such as "possessed of charm"; and "sweet of love". She must have had a low sweet voice too, which one would expect with her hesitant but warm smile and sensitive mouth. Akhenaten expressed it as "one is happy to hear her voice" and she "contents the Aten with her sweet voice". A musical and charming voice was an asset also emphasised by those who wrote about Cleopatra. One of Nefertiti's titles was that of 'Heiress', although we have no word that she was the daughter of a king. Possibly Akhenaten meant, when he had her thus described, that she was to be his heiress, his successor if the fates decreed; and it seems they did. Everything in the scenes carved in his reign, illustrates, as will be seen, just how he viewed her and how he meant the people of the country to view her as his Regnant Queen. Their mutual devotion is made unmistakably obvious to us today in the hundreds of scenes carved and painted of them together, especially at Amarna where they are almost never shown apart. They shared their state lives as well as their home and family and such harmony could hardly be so vividly commemorated if it had not existed. It was a true partnership.

The scene which first shows them to us together is carved on the walls of the tomb of the statesman - Vizier Ramose. There are a number of clues in it which show how early it is in their marriage. One is they were apparently still childless, as very soon and forever after their daughters begin to appear with them in practically every scene of the hundreds that were carved: first the eldest princess, Meritaten; then five more. As none is here we can make a pretty 'sure guess' that none was born because even when they were babies they were 'projected' with a forward look, as little girls with their parents. Another clue, and in archaeology every hint matters, Nefertiti stands demurely behind her husband in a window, not even fully shown, as they 'appear' to the people. Akhenaten leans forward acknowledging the acclaim, 'taking the salute' as it were; nothing unusual in that. But *very* unusually Nefertiti stands so unacclaimed, holding a drooping queenly lily. After the birth of Meritaten, Nefertiti is shown again and again *participating* with Akhenaten or alone, officiating as his equal. Another very obvious sign of the early date is that in the inscriptions neither of them has changed their names to include the Aten. Very early in the reign Akhenaten changed his inherited throne name Amenophis IV to Akhenaten meaning 'in the Spirit of the Aten', the name of the god in whose 'spirit' they lived. It was probably shortly after Meritaten was born, or even at her birth that Nefertiti added an 'Aten' name in front of her own. Her name 'Nefertiti' means 'A Beautiful Woman has Come'; and in front of that she added 'Nefernefruaten', meaning 'Beautiful are the Beauties of the Aten'. Her full name, NefernefruatenNefertiti, is shown everywhere in the thousands of inscriptions from the time it was changed in Thebes for nearly the whole length of the reign in Amarna.

In Ramose's tomb we can also see the beginning of many other surprising things which make this reign unique. This couple, even in the traditionally inclined ancient Egypt, dared to be so different that even today some people are incredulous when they see the innovations they introduced. In the scenes carved on the walls early in the decoration of the tomb, the elegant, rather static style of art remained as it had been for hundreds of years. Then, when Akhenaten's new ideas reached the artists, the idea of 'movement' was introduced into the pictures, reflecting the new philosophy. For instance the roof is left open above the King and Queen so that their sun-god could shine directly down upon them, with a hand to bless them on the end of each of its golden rays. These were entirely new features in Egyptian thought and art. The sun as a god had been worshipped for thousands of years, even before the pyramids were built, particularly at Heliopolis in the Delta. But never had the Aten been worshipped as the only creator of all living things, as it was during the life of Akhenaten and Nefertiti. This scene acknowledging the new element is one of the first indications left to us of its development in Thebes, before it reached its height in their new city of Amarna. This they dedicated to the Aten. In Ramose's tomb, the god is still connected with Horus the hawk-god and Re (Ra), the very early sun-god. Ultimately, only Re remained as 'the Father' with Aten as the disc of the sun.

Fig. 2. *Ankh* (sign of 'life')

Everywhere at Thebes and at Amarna, the sun's rays are shown bringing the *Ankh*, (Fig. 2) the sign of 'Life' to the King and Queen and only to them. There is one exception at Amarna, when as 'crowned heads' Akhenaten's mother and father are shown receiving this divine gift. Not content with blessing them with this immortal gift, in Ramose's tomb a hand of the Aten can be seen resting gently in blessing upon the Queen's shoulder, while another blesses the *uraeus* on her brow - that powerful and protective image of a cobra poised to strike. This is worn as a royal sign of power only by kings and their 'Great' queens ('Great' meaning the chief or principal queen, not a concubine or secondary wife). Other hands of the Aten bless the King's crown and even support his arm. The action in this 'new' art is shared even by the god itself, and the close association of god, King and Queen is continued throughout the reign. The image of a trinity grows, until later on, the actual prayers and petitions are offered to all three equally. But we go ahead too fast. Here another innovation is shown giving equality to the royal pair - both often wear the same type of clothes; pleated robes, sometimes with a shoulder wrap. Later, and even more historically important, they both wear the same type of kingly crowns. In the robes the differences are mainly those of sex, because although Nefertiti's gowns are usually open down the front, Akhenaten is always shown wearing a man's hip-wrap, pleated horizontally and secured by a king's belt with a tie

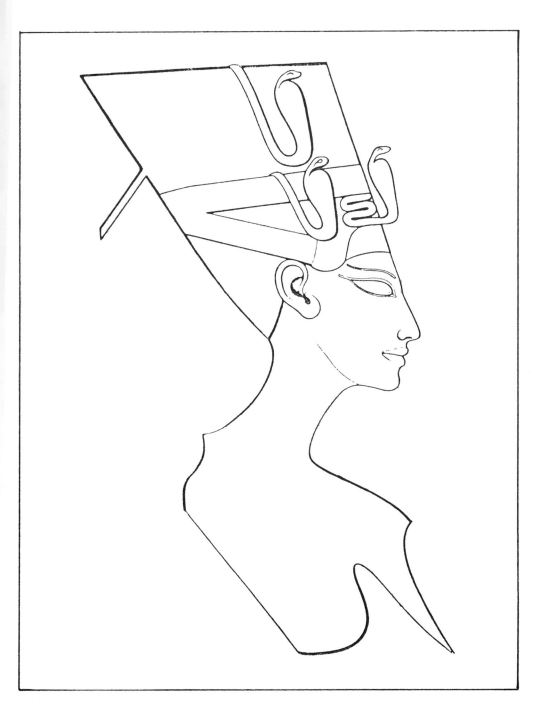

Fig. 3. Drawing of Nefertiti from a window scene at Amarna

hanging down the centre-front weighted with ornaments. In this age, unlike that of Cleopatra's from which we have fascinating detailed accounts, we depend on observation and it is to scenes like this one that we turn for our facts.

Clearly Nefertiti was a woman of distinction. (Fig. 3) She was elegant in her poise and person; demonstrably loving and unashamed of being thus shown; gracefully gowned and the only queen to initiate a becoming crown for herself. The tall, straight-edged head-dress by which she is so well-known, is blue, an echo of the 'blue' *Khepresh* or 'war' crown worn by kings, which Akhenaten frequently wore, made with a soft rather bonnet-like effect. Both were covered with the little round discs which, on the 'war crown' were thought originally to have been made of metal, hard enough to deflect arrows in a battle. There were no wars in this reign as such: but working one day in the Petrie Museum, we found fragments of glazed-ware crowns which were covered in discs like a king's 'blue' crown,. but which were in fact from portraits and statues of Nefertiti. Her crown in Fig. 3 is without the discs but shows the unique shape she chose to wear constantly, entwined with the power of the royal cobras.

Nefertiti's full name - NefernefruatenNefertiti - is written as one name in the 'cartouche', the oval ring, which surrounds the royal name of every king and 'Great' queen. The change may even have been made by a royal proclamation, as for a king. Names were of great importance to the bearer of them in ancient Egypt. Everyone's main hope was for an 'eternal life', to spend as they did this one (how they loved life), and to achieve this their own name had to be 'spoken', to be 'called' after their death. So the defamation or withdrawal of a person's name was the worst thing that could happen to them. We shall use 'Nefertiti', the Queen's short name in this book, because it is the one by which she is so well-known. But she would not have been spoken of thus at Amarna, where NefernefruatenNefertiti was written everywhere, automatically. *Because* her full name was not used in the early days of Egyptology and she was always spoken and written of just as 'Nefertiti', her Aten name 'Nefernefruaten' became separated from her, and attached to the fictitious figure of a royal youth, of whose existence there is absolutely no authenticated evidence. This guess was hazarded nearly 100 years ago and has never been proved. In view of the supreme importance of a person's name to the owner, Akhenaten would never have allowed this name of hers to be used by another except to be carried on by one of their daughters as Nefernefruaten-the-younger. Furthermore there is no identifiable royal figure such as this hypothetical youth on any of the monuments. In fact, no one other than Nefertiti is shown with the attributes necessary for a successor to Akhenaten. The perpetuation of this unsubstantiated guess made so long ago, without evidence, has muddled the history of the royal family, which was not corrected, as will be seen, until the 1970s.

16

II   Nefertiti as a Leader

The story and the speed of the developments in Nefertiti's status in Thebes is astonishing. This beautiful Queen, mother of the royal children, was carved with the King in colossal statues in the city architecture. This was unique except for queen monarchs. She is shown on gateways, in great scenes on pillars, on temple pylons and in temple wall scenes. Even more remarkable she is shown worshipping the Aten in kingly style, at altars with the King, or alone, or sometimes with her daughter(s). Small wonder if the people gasped in wonderment. Even the powerful 'Great Queens' of the past did not play such an important role and were often shown knee-high to the King in statues, although as Queen-Monarch, Hatshepsut was of course carved in kingly style on state buildings. Some people, when these scenes were first unearthed, imagined that Nefertiti was a goddess in the service of the Aten. But the revered and ancient goddesses did not play a regal role with the kings. Their roles were in the temples, blessing the kings, and sometimes the queens, but naturally not placed in cities as regal figures, nor shown as the mother of a king's six daughters.

Akhenaten had the example before him of his father, Amenophis III, dauntlessly choosing as his 'Great Royal Wife' a woman who was not of royal descent but from a family at Court, a fact he literally flaunted by issuing many large inscribed 'news' scarabs or 'special editions', which they certainly were, annoucing her parentage and saying that Ty was his Chief Royal Wife. He circulated the news widely, at home and abroad in the countries where Egypt's influence was great during this period of a virtual Empire. This much loved Queen, Ty, Akhenaten's mother, was greatly honoured, but never shown as a king, or in roles other than those which could be expected of a 'Great' Queen. Late in his reign, Amenophis had a lake made for Queen Ty by their palace on the West Bank of the Nile, opposite the town of Thebes. He announced this on one of his large 'news scarabs' and launched a boat for her which was named 'The Aten Gleams'. One can imagine that this name was chosen by their son and heir, Akhenaten, when he saw the boat skimming across the sparkling water and gleaming in the sun as it reflected his dream of worshipping only the Aten out of all the hundreds of other gods in ancient Egypt.

The art of Amarna reflects an age respecting 'truth' - the word that was part of the phrase that became virtually a royal motto, 'living in truth'. Wrongly quoted as he usually is, Oliver Cromwell did say to his portrait painter Lely, "Remark all . . . warts and everything as you see me, otherwise I will never pay a farthing for it" (his portrait!). This we know was not the attitude in Thebes or at Amarna, but we have the words of Akhenaten's chief sculptor Bek, who goes down in history as having said that the King was his 'teacher' and although this may have an element of flattery in it, it does show Akhenaten's involvement in the artistic break-through that occurred. He and Nefertiti freed the inimitable skills of the Egyptian artists from having to carve their royal figures as perfect, ageless images. From this freedom flowed the gaiety and liveliness of Amarna art, instead of the more stereotyped gestures and conventions of the past. It is well-known that art students are apt to impose their own familiar mental picture upon their drawing or - exaggerate the differences. The Egyptian sculptors at first exaggerated what must have been to them an almost blasphemous attempt to display the King and Queen as they were, instead of idealising them as ageless and impassive. Lines were accentuated and shapes over-emphasised. This can be seen when comparing some of the earlier portraiture with the later naturalism of Amarna portraits, which are unsurpassed in world art. No other pharaoh has left us a record of his family in their own home, like the pictures we have from the lives of this family, which mirror the age. No other pharaoh but Akhenaten would have allowed his father, the powerful overlord of many lands, builder of many temples, father of many children, to be shown near the end of his life, not with the ageless impassiveness of past (and future) pharaohs, but fat, even listless on a throne beside his beautiful, alert looking wife, Queen Ty.

Nefertiti's looks must have been a delight and stimulus to the artists who drew, carved and painted her in so many different poses. They must have had models of her. But for them to capture her vitality and immortalise her beauty as they did, she must have sat for them at times so they could observe her at close quarters and from every angle. She and her daughters mostly wore open coat-frock dresses of sheer, transparent material, clearly without any inhibitions about showing their bodies, so no 'bikinis'. Nefertiti is pictured in Thebes in front of an Aten altar, where she stands young, lissom and graceful in her long dress, which is transparent except for the pleats in its gossamer thinness and has a red sash falling nearly to her small sandalled feet. The altar is laden with poultry, bread, and the fruit and flowers of the countryside, with bowls of flaming incense on top of it to send fragrance up to the sun whose rays come down to bless her face and body. (Fig. 4)

It is historically significant that she is shown having abandoned the traditional woman's role in a temple of making music by ringing a sistrum, a hand-sized metal musical rattle. Instead she raises her arms to the god, as Akhenaten does, and offers a model of Maat, the goddess of 'truth' and 'rightness' which is traditionally a king's offering in a temple. On the altar is a model wearing the

Fig. 4. Nefertiti's and the god's name on altar

same tall, plumed head-dress on a coronet as Nefertiti is wearing herself. What a change from the earlier picture of her with Akhenaten. Behind her now stands the eldest princess Meritaten, who could have been little more than a baby or toddler at the time, but who is shown as a little girl ringing a sistrum, which is how she and her sisters were perpetually pictured. Above her is the formal description repeated so many times with each princess's name:

"Daughter of the King, Beloved of his body, Meritaten,
born of the Great Wife of the King, Nefertiti, may she
live eternally."

In this stereotyped inscription the Queen's early short name 'Nefertiti' is
carved: but in the later development on the altar where her name, and *only* her
name appears with that of the god and without Akhenaten's, her full name
Nefernefruaten-Nefertiti is carved. Another instance of her full name being
placed alone with the god is in a continuous inscription on a stone frieze. It
recurs between the names of the Aten, and she is described with the god as a
ruler in the phrase "adoration by all the people of the Aten and Nefernefruaten-
Nefertiti". The word 'adoration' or 'praise' is one normally reserved for a god
or pharaoh, that is, the god incarnate. Her religious and regal importance is also
vividly stressed in scenes on the pillars in a courtyard of a temple. They are
now called the 'Nefertiti Pillars'! (Fig. 5)

On three sides of the pillars, in scenes up to their full height, she is shown
ringing two sistrums at an altar, with Meritaten behind her, ringing one! But on
the fourth side, the latest to be carved, comes the unmistakable 'new look'.
Nefertiti is again shown not practising the women's ringing ritual but raising her
arms in offering and 'adoration'. No one could miss this repetitive emphasis of
her distinction. A very remarkable inscription in this and other Aten scenes in
Thebes is the feminisation of the usual phrase "He who Found the Aten" to
"She who Found the Aten". We have no proof that it was Nefertiti who had
the idea of simplifying the worship of this one creative god, but of course it
could have been so. In any case, the King and Queen were equally connected
with it, which is proved by later inscriptions of the prayers being addressed
equally to them both. Nowhere else is a queen, however 'Great' described as
the equal of a pharaoh, unless she was a pharaoh, as Hatshepsut was when she
brought her younger brother to be her co-regent.

Women in ancient Egypt enjoyed equality under the law, and those in
eminent positions had rich possessions and privileges. The 'Great' wives of the
pharaohs, for instance, had their own palaces. In the days of the pyramid
builders they even had their own pyramid as a tomb. The famous Queen
Hetepheres (Hetep-heres), daughter of a pharaoh, wife of a pharaoh, and mother
of the Pharaoh Cheops, who built the largest pyramid of them all in about
2,500 B.C., had beautiful gold-embellished furniture in her palace, and her gold
and silver jewels were exquisitely patterned with inlays of lapis lazuli, turquoise
and carnelian. Those objects which were able to be rescued from her grave, despite it being robbed and desecrated in her own time, have been restored and are
a joy to be seen in the Cairo Egyptian Museum. Other 'Great' queens enjoyed
cults with their husband or their son. Akhenaten's mother, Queen Ty, was

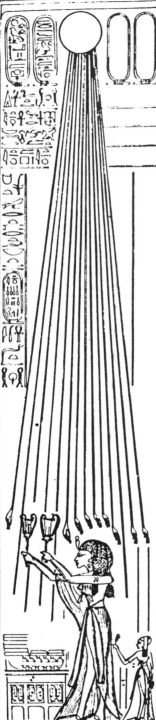

Fig. 5. A 'Nefertiti Pillar',
Karnak

21

known at home and abroad for her influence, so it was not such a far cry for Akhenaten to continue the trend and increase the status of his 'beloved' Queen. But he went much further. Only NefernefruatenNefertiti has been found recorded with regnant qualities by the side of her pharaoh-husband in his lifetime, and, with relatively new finds we can now see more carvings immortalising her regality. Akhenaten probably found it necessary to emphasise to the enriched and entrenched priesthood of the god Amen in Thebes, the unequivocal nature of the position she held. Here was not a goddess but a Regnant Queen. The determined and powerful purpose is obvious behind the numerous carvings, and they spell aloud that Akhenaten wanted no mistake made! He was writing and displaying in the various carved scenes the new social and religious development as well as showing to his people his wife's equality at his side. In Thebes this policy was pictured many years before their co-rule was actually recorded at Amarna, where it was subsequently celebrated by officially linking his name with her Aten name 'Nefernefruaten'. They were both carved together as in a co-regency.

When this King and Regnant Queen drove out amongst their people in Thebes, they passed through the huge beflagged pylons and gateways with the carved colossal figures of themselves towering into the blue Egyptian sky. In these statues Nefertiti was of relative size to Akhenaten (not knee-high nor sitting at his feet) and her gowns, her wigs and even her sandals were carved carefully with loving detail. This equal portrayal of a young Queen in such corresponding proportions and importance to the colossi of a king on monuments of a capital city is unknown in Egypt, even long after this period. The 'Beloved' 'Great' Queen of Rameses II, Queen Nefertari (Nefer-tari) clings to the pharoah's foreleg and reaches only to his knee in many statues, in fact all, except those on the façade of her *own* temple at Abu Simbel, beside his monstrous colossi.

As well as the colossal statues of Akhenaten from the destroyed Aten temple at Karnak, on all of which he wears a man's hip-wrap, there is also one colossal statue from there of a nude figure *without* the wrap and without male genitalia being carved. Curiously this was described at first as 'asexual' but it is now recognised as female! The breasts are carved more like those of a woman, although Akhenaten was plump-chested. It must have been one of several colossal statues of Nefertiti. There are fragments of others like it. Presumably this nude feminine figure was to have been finished as Nefertiti, wearing her open robe and the tall crown of kings of a united Egypt, a part of which remains on the statue. These feminine statues, so different from Akhenaten's, were differently vandalised from his. There must have been considerable jealousy of this regnant queen, and of her partnership with Akhenaten in worshipping the Aten, and of them both using the money in the overflowing Amen coffers to build

Aten temples, and finally, even a new capital city dedicated to the Aten. The idea of a queen ruling with her husband did not occur easily to the Egyptians. It has not occurred easily to Egyptologists. But now we have pictures of Nefertiti wearing kings' crowns when she is *with* her husband. Our own Queen Mary II was a Regnant Queen in the 17th century A.D., although she was married to King William III.

Travellers today can see the remains of the huge temples at Karnak, which were dedicated to the god Amen-Re, and administered by the immensely powerful Amen priesthood. Akhenaten's father built a very beautiful one at Luxor dedicated to Amen-Re. But nothing of the Aten temple built at Karnak was left standing. The fundamental information of Nefertiti's status in the early years of the reign was only found in the 1960's, when the carved scenes from the Aten temple were unearthed. During the course of his reign Akhenaten concentrated more and more on the Aten as the sole creator and finally suppressed the worship of Amen and other gods, but particularly Amen whose monuments he eventually had defaced or destroyed.

Tutankhamen who followed Akhenaten's successor, returned to Thebes from Amarna and restored Amen worship, but he did not destroy Aten buildings and iconography. It was probably some 100 years or so later, in the time of the kings named Rameses, that the worst damage was perpetrated. Not only were the Aten temples in Thebes destroyed and buried away in the pylons of later temples, but Amarna itself was plundered for stone, wrecked to the ground, and the building stones ferried across the river to Hermopolis (the modern town of Ashmunein) for the buildings there of Rameses II and others. Many of these Amarna blocks from Thebes have been collected and their pictures published, and more ancient stone blocks are now being found by the British Museum dig at Ashmunein. But the beautiful city of Amarna was completely destroyed, over 3,000 years before the modern bomb.

Some Aten temple blocks have been found from time to time at Luxor, but only in 1966 was modern search and research begun on a momentous scale. 35,000 building blocks, sometimes called by the Arabic word *talatat*, were rescued from their burial in the pylons; and were photographed, coded, computerised, and matched wherever possible by the University Museum of Pennsylvania with the Organisation of Egyptian Antiquities. These finds have revolutionised our knowledge of the earliest years of the reign. One set of these building blocks, for instance, have been fitted together to display in a series of pictures what they originally showed on the temple walls - a stone-carved strip-story of the most outstanding religious festival in Egyptian religious life, the *Heb Sed* or 'Jubilee Festival'. This was designed for the reinforcement and renewal of the pharaoh's powers by the gods and was held at different times in different reigns. The Queen-Monarch Hatshepsut celebrated one in her fifteenth year. Its function is related entirely to the reigning pharaoh, and it looks in this case to have been associated with two pharaohs.

A procession is always part of the ceremony, and in this record two people, surely monarchs, are involved, which is unique. Nefertiti was not just slipped into the proceedings as part of the procession, which would have been extraordinary enough for a queen; she is prominently featured. The scenes show the departure of the two Kings together from the palace, Akhenaten wearing the typical short cloak usual for this affair, and Nefertiti in an unusually long, straight dress for her, with long sleeves - all-enveloping rather than her usual revealing open-fronted gown, presumably for this religious service. But, the most remarkable record is that of Nefertiti in the centre row of the series, where she is shown in a palanquin surrounded by kingly symbols in the manner of a pharaoh. (Fig. 6) Akhenaten's carrying chair, carved with striding lions and crowned sphinxes, is paralleled by Nefertiti's carved with striding lionesses and sphinxes mounted *in her own image*. They wear the double plumes of her typical head-dress at this time, as she does herself; and it is her head-dress again that is worn in the heraldry of the surrounding royal cobras. The watching crowds must have been overawed by the sight of the Queen who was not only included in this Festival, but made such a prominent part of it. She was displayed in her own palanquin - state carriage of the day - surrounded by courtiers and officials,

Fig. 6. Nefertiti carried in *Heb Sed* procession

24

The reason that Nefertiti was bedecked with symbols of royal power in such a significant procession suggests Akhenaten's dynamic policy to stress her regality. This would have been viewed as daring by 'Church and State' and have made the people rub their eyes to make sure they were seeing straight. In one row of pictures Nefertiti is shown leaving her palanquin. Surrounded by bowing courtiers, she enters a temple, possibly her own, alone. In the next picture the courtiers are shown still bowing, but left outside. In the procession the three little princesses, of whom the third could scarcely have been more than a baby in arms, are shown as three identical adults in three identical carrying chairs. This obvious example of a forward-look from childhood to maturity is not unique in Egyptian royal history.

What could be called the final seal of Nefertiti's regality, was carved in scenes of her in the pharaonic 'warrior' role before she left Thebes, and again in the same role at Amarna. These show her unequivocably as a 'Warrior King' subduing the enemies of Egypt: see Fig. 7. *Only* pharaohs are ever found pictured in this conqueror's role throughout the whole of Egyptian history. Ever since Narmer, about 3,000 B.C., *only kings,* and those repeatedly, have been illustrated in this symbolic striding stance of a sovereign towering over an enemy captive (or captives in a row) held by the hair and about to be killed by a blow from a club or scimitar held high in a swinging gesture by the pharaoh. But in Thebes it is Nefertiti who is shown (in different gowns and head-dresses) performing this *coup-de-grace* over a captive. Wearing her own particular blue crown found for the first time in her reign, she strides towards the captive and is shown similarly to all pharaohs performing this ritual. She grasps the enemy by the hair and swings the scimitar over her head on its fateful journey towards the prisoner. Nefertiti was essentially feminine in her ways and dress except in this wholly symbolic scene of her kingship.

Fig. 7. Nefertiti as a 'Warrior King'

In another panel she is shown wearing a long dress and on her head the disc and high plumes over her coronet (feminine as could be) but still the orders had gone forth to show her unmistakably in this pharaonic heraldry. In the central panel between these two, she wears the disc and plumes on her head but is a sphinx trampling on the enemy. The Great Queen Ty, her mother-in-law, was shown as a sphinx, a human-headed lioness couchant, but *holding up the name of her husband the pharaoh,* and not appearing in the subjugating role of a pharaoh herself. This essentially kingly image (for that is clearly what it is) pictures Nefertiti not in a battle but as a ruler. It is almost possible to hear Akhenaten saying - let there be no mistake; Nefertiti must be seen to be a regal queen, so show her in this unmistakable scene.

Another example of Nefertiti in this role, is carved on those blocks of stone from Amarna which were found across the river at Hermopolis. It is significant that on one of these blocks, the scene is carved on the outside of a Nile boat. What better way could there be to spread the news throughout the land and to travellers in Egypt, than that the Queen should be shown as a king in this specific pose of world overlordship, on the outside of a Nile boat? This head-line news must have spread like wildfire. The fact that Akhenaten was shown in the same typical gesture on a boat in an *adjacent* scene would have scotched any rumour that she was supplanting him or even trying to, and it would have explained that this was a regal partnership - a co-rule.

To take such exhaustive trouble to show Nefertiti in this role parallel with her husband's kingship, shows the strength of purpose that lay behind the aim to show her as a pharaoh. On the boat where she is thus displayed, she is again wearing her own unmistakable crown, and a belted topless skirt like a king, but loose enough to allow the unusually masculine stride she has to take. (Fig. 7) This block from Hermopolis, showing Nefertiti engaged in this unusual scene on the outside of a royal craft, found its way to America. Good gracious, people said, the beautiful Nefertiti must have been a horrid woman! But Dr. John Cooney, then of the Brooklyn Museum, who was the first to publish it in his book on *Amarna Reliefs in American Collections* in 1965, saw not only the past, but looked into the future. "Why," he wrote, "was this famous Queen shown in this function always reserved for the king? If she were Queen Regnant, the composition, still exceptional, would be understandable or even suitable, but as Queen Consort the role is unique and incongruous." It would be; even ridiculous. But his far-sightedness preceded the discoveries in the 1970s when the evidence that establishes Nefertiti *as* a Queen Regnant was being recognised for the first time.

To explain the changes wrought by Akhenaten and Nefertiti in the religion, would first need a whole book to describe the complexities of the many cults that had grown up during the thousands of years of Egyptian history. The complications were immense because of the hundreds of gods and goddesses that existed: animal, human and a blend of both, with aspects, powers and responsibilities that merged, and changed with the period, and with the locality of the different regimes. Many were local; some were national. The sun itself, was a god worshipped as far back as prehistoric times, before the texts were inscribed on the walls of the pyramids. But it was represented in various ways:

Khepri, the morning sun, was portrayed as a scarab beetle, sometimes shown as a man with a scarab beetle as a head, and at other times just the beetle within the sun's disc; Re (sometimes spelt Ra) was for long looked upon as the noon-day sun and shown as a man with a hawk's head wearing a sun's disc. The evening sun was sometimes shown as Aten - the sun's disc, or as Re-Atum who was portrayed as a man. The great goddess Isis was mother of Horus the falcon, much connected with the power of kings; (she was also shown suckling Horus as a human child); then the sun and Horus mingled as Re-Horakhti, Horus of the Horizon. Osiris was the god of the underworld for centuries and also connected with re-birth and fertility; Min, the phallic god of Coptos was also connected with reproduction - and so on. The ancient goddess Hathor defied all time and borders. She is sometimes shown as a divine, benign cow; sometimes as a woman with heifer's ears and a head-dress with a cow's horns, or just a wig; sometimes disguised as a sycamore tree with a breast suckling kings, as in Figure 18, at other times she is carved as a woman. Amongst the animal gods and goddesses to be looked to for happiness and benefits or sometimes feared, were cats and crocodiles, lionesses and snakes; hippopotami, birds, bulls and baboons.

At no other time did anything approach the utter simplification of one creator as introduced by Akhenaten and Nefertiti, in place of the massive complexities that had gone before and followed after. Their thought was an intellectual break-through; a peak of clarity which rose above the lowlands of superstition that had existed until then. They swept aside all but the sun's disc as sole creator. They revered the attributes of the goddess Maat, a woman who wore an upright feather in her head-dress, and she was often invoked by them for her elements of truth, rightness and order. But these were moral concepts, rather than benefits to be gained from a deity to whom one applied for life and protection. There is no sign in the Amarna royal tomb of the underworld Osiris-rites, i.e., the rituals for the next world. *But*, there was complete freedom for the people to worship their gods of old. There was toleration for all gods except the powerful Amen-of-Thebes who is rarely found amongst the multiplicity of deities reproduced for the people at Amarna.

In the glass and glazing factories, Petrie found hundreds and thousands of beads, rings (even small enough for the children); jewels and amulets of all the ancient deities, human, and animal and a combination of both. All the symbols against evil and for luck and good fortune were made for everyone to own and wear and treasure in their homes. They were found even in the workmen's village in the desert. Petrie brought back thousands of them, with the red clay moulds in which they were shaped and then fired for glazing. They can be seen in the Petrie Museum today retaining all their colours enjoyed in the 14th century B.C., red, bright blue, greens, yellow and white. They were worn as adornments as well as religious talismen. But Akhenaten must have seen the power of the priesthood of Amen growing and threatening the political balance of the country. He was something of a prophet, for in about 1,000 B.C., a High Priest of Amen actually took the title of King at Thebes! But to appreciate fully the radiance of the belief of Akhenaten and Nefertiti in the Aten, their Poem to the God in the next chapter must be read. It is translated from the hieroglyphs in which it is carved on the stone walls in the cliff tombs of Amarna.

III   Breakaway City of the Aten

The tremendous change in the religious thought of Akhenaten and Nefertiti has been called a revolution. Unfortunately in Europe this word has unhappy associations with bloodshed, the guillotine, or burning at the stake. Nothing could be more different from their benign and tolerant regime under their chosen creator the Aten.

They must have built their Aten temples at Thebes open to the sun: roofless for its blessing to descend on to the worshippers. This idea alone surely seemed sacrilegious to the orthodox when compared with the progressive gloom in the traditional temple pattern, which increases in darkness from the front courtyards throughout the building until one reaches the Holy-of-Holies which is almost blacked out. In this the priest and/or king, only and alone, attended to the daily religious rites. But in Thebes the sun-filled Aten temples were still physically part of the more ancient buildings wrapped in priestly mysteries; still in the capital soaked in the worship of Amen-Re and mythologies of the many gods of the past; still under the watchful if not envious and disbelieving eyes of the Amen and other priesthoods.

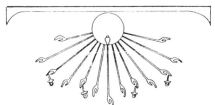

Fig. 8. The Aten sun-disc

It is small wonder that the imagination of the royal couple was stimulated to start afresh. Avoiding the word revolution, their decision was a stupendous change. Their venture was a bold one: to build a new capital city in the desert away from the usual gods and dedicated to only one, and illumined throughout by the rays from this creator, the sun's disc, the Aten. This needed courage and to understand fully the impetus for the breakaway and the spirit that infused it, perhaps the best way is to look at the radiance in their Praise to the Aten.

Poem of Praise to the Sun

You arise beauteous in the horizon of the heavens
Oh living Aten who creates life.
When you shine forth in the Eastern horizon you fill every land
    with your beauty.
You are so beautiful: you are great; gleaming and high over
    every land.
Your rays embrace the lands and all you have created;
You are Re and reach out to all your creations, and hold them
    for your beloved Son.
You are afar, but your rays touch the earth;
Men see you, but know not your ways.

When you set in the Western horizon of the sky
The earth is in darkness like the dead.
People sleep in their rooms with covered heads;
They do not see each other.
If all their possessions were stolen
They would know it not.
Every lion leaves its lair;
All snakes bite;
Darkness covers all.
The world is silent
For the creator rests in his horizon.

When you rise from the horizon the earth grows bright;
You shine as the Aten in the sky and drive away the darkness;
When your rays gleam forth, the whole of Egypt is festive.
People wake and stand on their feet
For you have lifted them up.
They wash their limbs and take up their clothes and dress;
They raise their arms to you in adoration.

Then the whole of the land does its work;
All cattle enjoy their pastures,
Trees and plants grow green,
Birds fly up from their nests
And raise their wings in praise of your spirit.
Goats frisk on their feet,

And all fluttering and flying things come alive
Because you shine on them.
Boats sail up and downstream,
All ways are opened because you have appeared.
The fish in the river leap up to you
Your rays are in the deep of the sea.

You are the creator of the issue in woman,
The seed in men;
You give life to the son in his mother's womb
Soothing him so he does not cry
Oh nurse within the womb.

You give the breath of life to all your creations
From the day they are born.
You open their mouths and give them sustenance.
To the chick that cries "tweet" while still in the egg
You give breath in the shell to let him live,
And make the time for him to break the shell
And come out of the egg at the moment for him to chirp
And patter on his two feet.

How manifold are your works: they are secret from our sight
Oh unique god, no other is like you.
You made the earth after your own heart
When you were alone. All men, herds
And flocks, all on the earth that goes on its feet,
and all that is in the sky and flies with its wings.
The land of Egypt, the foreign lands of Syria and Nubia too -
You put every man in his place and fulfil his needs;
Each one with his sustenance and the days of his life counted,
Their language is different,
And they look different;
Their complexions are different,
For you have distinguished the nations.
You make the seasons to bring into being all your creatures;
Winter to cool them,
And the heat of summer to come from you.
You have made the sky afar off
So when you rise you can see all you have made.
You alone rise in the form of the living Aten

Shining afar, yet close at hand.
You make millions of forms out of you alone,
Towns and villages, fields, roads and river.
All eyes see you before them
For you are the Aten of the day, over all the earth.

You are in my heart and none other knows thee
But your son "Akhenaten";
You have given him understanding of your designs and your power.
The people of the world are in your hand
Just as you have created them.
All men since you have made the earth you have raised for your son
Who came forth from your body,
The King of Egypt who lives in truth,
Lord of Diadems, Akhenaten, whose life is long:
And for his beloved wife
Mistress of Two Lands, NefernefruatenNefertiti
May she live and flourish in eternity.

The poem has often been compared with Psalm 104. The psalm was written some 500 years later. This was the ideal to which they wanted to dedicate their new capital city and in about the fourth year of his reign, Akhenaten set out with his retinue to find a site away from Thebes. They drove north, their horses galloping over the sands with the sun's rays shimmering through the clouds of dust raised by their chariot wheels, and bivouaced in the desert at night. Finally, on the east side of the Nile, they came to a desert plain that was surrounded by a semi-circle of high cliffs. It had never been built on; never dedicated to any god or goddess and Akhenaten felt the Aten had revealed the place to him. It was about halfway between the old capital Thebes and the northern city of Memphis (near Cairo), and conveniently some 200 miles from the ancient cults. It was also conveniently near the oasis of the Fayum where Akhenaten's mother, Queen Ty, had a palace.

But apart from its position, the distinction of the site makes the choice understandable: it is enchanting. The protection of the encircling cliffs gives the plain a hushed seclusion and a nature entirely of its own, and here they built one of the most remarkable cities of the ancient world. If today one climbs up the sliding, sandy slopes to the tombs of the courtiers and officials carved high in the cliffs, and turns to look back over the plain, one can feel its fascination: remote but not lonely; isolated, but not stark; with an area of desert wide enough to build the city between the cliffs and the river, with more land on the other side of the Nile to keep the herds and crops.

Looking down on to the bare outlines of its once beautiful buildings, with only the occasional two or three feet of mud brick left standing, there is a haunting echo of what a lovely, lively city it must have been and a sadness for its dreadful destruction. The grandeur of the valley scenery behind the cliffs, where the royal tomb is cut in a ravine, is indescribably majestic; and high up in the cliffs themselves, north and south of the royal ravine, are the noblemen's tombs with columned entrances and several rooms cut into the rock. The walls were beautifully decorated with the carved and painted scenes, not all finished, but describing the life at Amarna. They have suffered from more than time. The tomb robbers and ransackers have hacked out great chunks of the scenes that displayed such a unique wealth of story and detail. There one can find revelations in the life of a royal family of a detailed intimacy not found anywhere else in the ancient world. And so many tombs so lovingly prepared for the officials and never used also seems extraordinary. Presumably the officials returned to Thebes when Tutankhamen moved his court back there at the death of Akhenaten and Nefertiti. Never has an epoch been so rounded off in but one generation.

The semi-circle of the cliffs marks an area about eight miles long, and in the centre it is three miles wide from the cliffs to the Nile. Akhenaten ordered huge inscriptions and scenes to be carved on the face of the cliffs of the eastern range and on the hills of the West Bank round the fields to mark the boundaries of the city. These monuments - the 'boundary stelae', are mostly carved with portraits of the royal family at the top, and inscribed with Akhenaten's vows to dedicate the site to the Aten. He called it *Akhetaten* meaning 'The Horizon of the Aten', the name 'Amarna' being a misunderstanding by early travellers of two Arabic names. The hieroglyphic inscriptions on the surfaces of the cliffs are now difficult or impossible to read from the ground, even with field-glasses, partly because of their height, partly from the weathering of the wind-blown sand over the centuries, and partly from modern wasps whose nests now half cover them. It is our good fortune that the tomb scenes were all copied nearly 100 years ago by Norman de Garis Davies, and remain for study in six volumes - *The Rock Tombs of El-Amarna.*

The area, Akhenaten stated, "belongs to Aten the Father: mountains, deserts, islands, upper and lower ground and water; villages, man and beasts and all things which the Aten my Father shall bring into existence, eternally, forever." It is as though he was clarifying that there would be no other god than the Aten, and no religious rituals as hitherto performed by the powerful priesthoods of the other religions. This unique distinction was undoubtedly respons-.ible for the destruction of his monuments. He vowed to build temples to the

Aten; palaces for himself and for the 'Great Royal Wife' NefernefruatenNefer-titi, with a tomb for them both in the hills, and for Meritaten their eldest daughter. She was probably the only one born when these great inscriptions were planned, although by the time all the monuments were carved, Nefertiti had given birth to two more princesses in Thebes, and the names and figures of her babies (as children) were being added to the inscriptions and to the statues of the family below them at the base of the cliff-face; eventually more tombs were prepared for them too.

Figure 9 gives an idea of the family in the early years, *before* the move to Amarna, while the stelae were being prepared. It is not from the exaggerated period. Akhenaten wears his typically rather bulging blue 'war' crown; his hip-wrap with a king's belt is weighted down the front by jewelled uraei. Nefertiti, young and lithe, wears her long flowing gown with a sash, but open down the front. Her graceful gesture to the Aten is unspoilt by the height of her head-dress mounted on the Theban styled wig, which she must have favoured when the plans were on the drawing board, because later, and especially at Amarna, she more often wore her unique, tall straight-sided crown. Whatever the height, width or weight of her regalia, she is always shown in a pose of gentle com-mand. The little princesses are wearing long gowns, with the side-lock of hair showing their youth; they are shaking their ever-present sistrums; but not Nefertiti. She, stepping forward, hails the god under its outstretched arms in the same way as Akhenaten. The Queen's full name is shown here as every-where in the hundreds of inscriptions at Amarna. There is one exception: the stela named 'K' by Petrie, where Nefertiti's full name and the news of the birth of her second daughter apparently did not reach the artists until they had nearly finished the carving, so that they had to add the figure of the second daughter, and the Queen's longer name *behind* her, after her figure, at the end of the inscription! The news could easily have taken months to reach the sculp-tors in the desert.

It would be impossible for us to say that NefernefruatenNefertiti was fear-less about the big move of her home and the capital. But we can see how un-inhibited her worship of the Aten was pictured in Thebes, against, almost cer-tainly amazement and disapproval of the new ideas. There must have been resentment of her power. But in this period, at the beginning of the change in the art when it could neither be called 'idealistic', nor the Queen presented as 'idealised', she was still always shown as a figure of strength and purpose. Nevertheless, this move to an unknown place was an adventurous undertaking. The young Queen had to go with her three small daughters and possibly an-other one on the way, some 200 miles down the Nile, to the unknown that was to be her home. It was an upheaval at best. She was to see her new home for the first time, the palaces, temples, the city buildings, tombs and monuments,

Fig. 9. Part of boundary stela with Akhenaten and Nefertiti worshipping the Aten. The two
princesses ring their sistrums

all being carved with countless scenes of her and her husband's lives together.
The craftsmen, stonemasons, the architects and artists and some of the courtiers had gone on before them, and the tillers of the land and herdsmen were on
the West Bank preparing produce to sail across to the city. But her confidence
in Akhenaten must have been immense and their belief and life-style completely shared.

On the royal boat for the journey, in a flotilla which must have accompanied them, it would have been comparatively quiet and peaceful, with little
more sound than that of their own voices, the flowing river, the breeze in a sail,
the plying of the oars, the singing of the crew, and the chatter of the children
as they ran from one side of the boat to the other to see the Egyptian palms
and other trees sliding by. The riverside crops and buildings in the changing
early and late lights and desert colours were like the scenes which Cleopatra

35

brought Caesar to enjoy a thousand years later, on a more luxurious and amorous journey up the Nile to Thebes.

Travelling to Amarna was a down-river journey, into whatever welcome cool air might come from the north, or any breeze before it fell, as it often did in the cool of the starlit nights. The attendants would be caring for the family and the court officials in this boat, while others in accompanying boats would be overseeing the crowns and regalia, the clothes and provisions. Probably Nefertiti's sisters were with her, and the great nobleman Ay with his famous wife Tey, and possibly Pentu who was chief physician to the King. These, and the officials who would meet them on arrival, were the statesmen who had their tombs carved in the cliffs, from which we have learnt so much.

But Nefertiti and her family could not have known what the city would be like and as the boat neared the shore must have been as amazed as the contemporary travellers were in those days, at the new city rising from the desert, with its large and magnificent buildings decorated by the finely carved stone hieroglyphs on them, large enough to be read from the river. Others gleamed with the brilliance of inlaid coloured glazes which made up whole pictures set into the walls. Fragments remain of the inlays from these scenes, not one of which, alas, Petrie found still in place. They had all fallen into the sand with the destruction of the walls of the city. There were the coloured figures and faces and the clothes and regalia from the palace scenes; inlaid fruit and flowers of the countryside; and piles of food on the laden Aten altars - all of glazed ware. They must have equalled if not surpassed the inlaid scenes in any other city in the ancient world. Petrie found the actual glass and glazing factories where the tens of thousands of these pieces of inlay and tiles (and the jewellery) were made. The volume must almost have equalled the dimension of the building itself, for the remains of these decorations had fallen not only from the once gleaming walls but also from doors, columns, and from many statues adorned with coloured glazes for the features, crowns and clothing.

As the boat drew near the shore it would have tied up eventually alongside the quay of the central 'official' palace, with its western wall stretching for some half a mile along the cooling river. When the King and Queen disembarked, perhaps with an oration to greet them, they would have been met by such officials as Apy, the Royal Scribe and Steward to the Household, and Mahu, Chief of Police to control the welcoming crowds. Then they would have been whirled in chariots around the north end of their huge palace, passing the Great Aten Temple on their left, and continuing into the 'royal road' to the gateway of their home. This was joined to the palace by a bridge over the road down which they had driven - the fly-over of antiquity. The children could have been taken to their house through the Broad Hall of the palace, open to the sky with the Aten shining down on it, and there they would have seen the

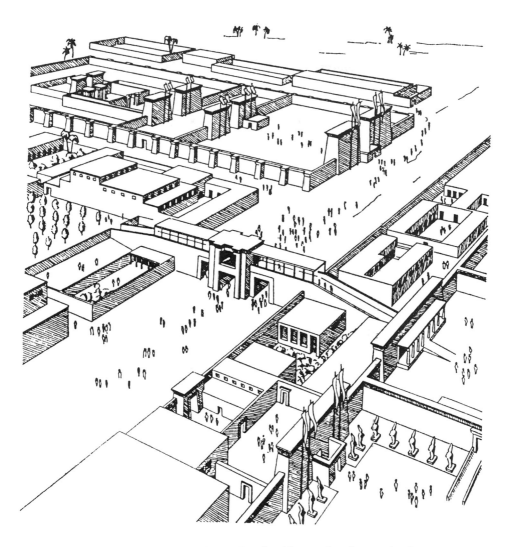

Fig. 10. The royal residence showing 'fly-over' and central palace
(reconstruction)

columns and the colossal statues of their parents, before the older ones could run up the ramp of the bridge and over it to their homes: see Figure 10. Travellers today can see the foundations of this very bridge, from which the family could look north and south over the city, and be seen as they crossed it by the people who were walking along the main highway underneath it, or driving through the big central archway. The sides of the bridge itself would be open for the cool north breeze to blow through and its walls were decorated with paintings of flowers and trees, which reflected the beauty of the garden of the royal home. The ramp leading down into this would have brought the children into their own terraced garden, with summer houses and potting sheds in the lower terrace, and an avenue of trees bordering the top terrace leading to the bridge. That the gardens themselves seem to have been formal in plan, is suggested by the patterns left in the sand of the little water channels made round the trees and plants, and the root-patterns themselves which had been packed round with plaster to keep the soil damp with the water which was brought from the river. When Akhenaten and Nefertiti reached their home their chariot would have been driven into a small courtyard beside the bridge and then into an inner court leading to the house.

IV　The Royal Home at Amarna

Akhenaten and Nefertiti entered their home through a series of ante-rooms which led to a great central room with forty-two painted wooden columns soaring up to its roof, and to the south side of that, another more intimate sitting-room with only twelve columns! The furnishing of these rooms was elegant and comfortable as we can see from a later painting of the family, which Petrie found when he was excavating the ruins. In this, the sixth little princess was only a baby sitting on her mother's lap. The walls and some ceilings were decorated with paintings, some religious, some of more ordinary daily happenings, and many of flowers. Although none of the city remains standing, it is clear that the family surrounded itself with scenes which express the beauty of nature.

In one corner of the royal house is a separate little 'suite' of six rooms which the excavator John Pendlebury, who continued the excavations long after Petrie's earlier work, believed could have been the princesses' night nurseries. Each little room had a small built-in niche at the back, usual in bedrooms for the bed itself to be made up of a soft mattress and fine linen. Surely these were the children's bedrooms which had to be increased in number as the princesses were born.

To get an idea of the furnishings of Akhenaten's and Nefertiti's bedroom and bathroom suites we have to draw on parallels from the city and other royal suites, for there was nothing left in the palace except outlines of the rooms and fragments of small objects saved by Petrie, and described later. One hopes that much was taken to Thebes by Tutankhamen and the third princess who became his wife, rather than they should have fallen into the hands of the looters. There were two large royal bedroom suites of several rooms, with bathrooms and lavatories. From one suite a door led into the garden; this was perhaps Akhenaten's, as the other was more sheltered, with access to it only through the inner courts and rooms, and therefore more suitable for Nefertiti. What she saw and thought when she went into her new bedroom for the first time we shall never know. Akhenaten would have carried out her every wish, and probably when she had time, after the excitement of the young people had subsided, her feeling would have been one of quiet pleasure. She would have been unlikely to have had less comfort and elegance than Queen Hetepheres had in the pyramid days. She more than probably also had a 'golden' bed, with carved lion's paws as feet, and an inlaid head-rest and foot-board, ready for the deep mattress and fine linen bed-clothes. Possibly there was, too, a high gold-covered frame to fit over three sides of the bed and a handsome bedside chair and table, all to be covered last thing at night (as the Great Queen Hetepheres' was) by a fine netting, for protection against insects.

The bathrooms and lavatories had screen walls overlapping at the entrance instead of having doors which would have shut out the air. Bathrooms in town houses often had a stone 'splash wall' behind the bath, but in the royal home it is probable that the bathrooms would have been lined with white limestone worked to the smoothness of marble. Baths were sometimes sunken into the floor for the attendants to pour the water and rinses over the bather, or raised on a platform, where there were ledges for the attendant to stand on, and emplacements for them on which to put the jugs of water. Towels would have been of linen or coarser cotton material, and there would have been plenty of perfumed oils. Akhenaten and Nefertiti would not have lacked bathing attendants with towels, and fans to cool them, and massage to rub in the fragrant oils on their bodies to protect the skin against the hot sun and desert winds. There must have been an elegant abundance of scented cosmetics. An early carving in the Louvre shows in one scene women picking and gathering lilies, and in another, squeezing them in a competent looking device for expressing the perfume for the scent bottles. Jars of fragrant scents and oils are amongst the precious things stolen from the tombs in antiquity, having been buried with their owners for their continued enjoyment in the next world, but taken by the robbers for their more immediate pleasure. Remembering the exquisite tiles Petrie found from the walls of Nefertiti's apartments in the palace opposite her home, it is easy to believe that the royal bathrooms had tiled floors, with runnels to take off the splashed water and convey it to drains outside.

The children apparently had a day nursery or play-room, with plenty of activities, some educational, to keep them busy and happy. Everywhere, in painted scenes, they saw around them lovely flowers, and when Pendlebury came across a room with paint brushes of palm fibre and drawing quills made of fish bones, the ends still stained with colour and a good deal of the raw paint streaked on the floor as though wiped off the brushes, he imagined this might have been from the young people's own efforts at painting. It was not just an excavator's dream: in Tutankhamen's tomb, a painter's palette belonging to the eldest princess Meritaten was found, with the brushes covered in the paint which had dried on them, and her own name engraved in the ivory.

As children, the little princesses, like many growing girls, doubtless tried out their mother's dressing-table equipment. We have, in the Petrie Museum, part of one of her perfume bottles. It was small enough to hold in the palm of the hand, and glazed royal blue. The shape of the broken piece still shows that it had a wide-spreading bowl to hold the scent and a narrow neck to minimise its evaporation. Nefertiti's name is inlaid in a delicate green and this colour was also used to shape a petalled necklace around the neck of the beautiful little container. Every picture carved and painted of the princesses shows their freedom to 'join in' with their parents; Nefertiti's ambience was clearly one of delight and freedom from undue restrictions.

As the princesses grew up they began to have their own cosmetic belongings, including tubes for kohl, that dark powder made from lead or antimony used by both men and women for eye-paint, as can be seen round the eyes of Tutankhamen and his Queen. (See Frontispiece) Petrie brought back a number of these tubes, which he found in the palace ruins. One in the Petrie Museum, made of a dark-red glaze is inlaid with Meritaten's name in white along the tube; another, a white one, has her name inlaid in the decorative blue powdered glass or 'frit'. The glazing of these small tubes, less than an inch in diameter, is technically perfect, the mastery giving just the right smoothness and shine to the surface of the lovely colours. Some of the green is a pure apple-green, with almost the colour-quality of Sèvres china. The sticks to insert in these narrow tubes to extract the eye-shadow are made of wood, glass or metal and have a wider flattened top to grip between thumb and forefinger and guide the eye-shadow in its application to lashes and eyebrows. One stick in the Museum is made of wood, with a metal spatula on the end as though for scraping the unused and perhaps dried kohl out of the narrow tubes. All the dishes for the scented oils and perfumes of great variety, and the other cosmetic objects used by both men and women for grooming, showed that imaginative attention was paid to their manufacture, so as to make them of beautiful shapes and colours. Some of the receptacles were finely carved in ivory; others in stone or painted wood; curlers, tweezers and razors had attractive leather cases, and one can imagine the sensuous enjoyment derived from handling these beautifully made objects used by the royal households and the landed population. Some of the tubular kohl pots were made of glass in the shape of a small hand-sized column with a spreading palm-leaf capital, with the column then decorated by bands of different coloured glass, dragged into loops around the stem while still warm and manageable.

A well-known design used in the XVIIIth Dynasty for perfume and ointment holders is that of the 'swimming girl'. (Pl. IV) They are so called because the carving is of a young girl lying face downwards with her arms outstreched in front - not, as might be thought to swim a breast stroke - but so she could hold a jar or bowl of cosmetics in her hands. Between the youthful shoulders of these horizontal figures, a hollow enabled the neck and head to be inserted vertically to look forward to the bowl held in the hands. These lovely little figures are made in stone, bone, wood and ivory, and an Amarna fragment in the Museum is made of alabaster. Despite the damage to it, the artist's superb skill can be seen in the skin-like surface and the details of the taut young body.

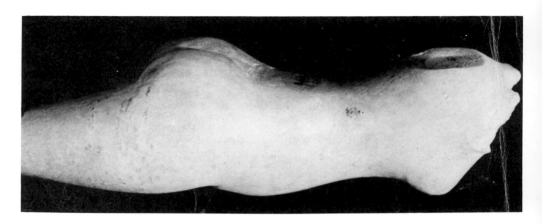

Plate IV. Perfume holder of 'swimming girl'

Hand-mirrors made of shining copper or bronze set in carved ivory or wooden handles would reflect the result of the wigs curled by the scissor-like metal curlers, no doubt heated for action. From the pictures it would seem that the aim of the make-up was to enhance natural beauty, rather than achieve a theatrical effect.

The elegance of the ancient Egyptians was not only skin-deep. They were personally fastidious as well as immaculately well groomed. Amongst the treasures rescued from the robbed and ransacked grave of Queen Hetepheres of the pyramid era, were her gold razors. The women of the Old Kingdom wore tight-fitting, clinging dresses fully revealing every shape of their bodies, and it would appear that these women's razors were used by them to remove pubic hair, and very probably under-arm hair too. From the gowns worn by Nefertiti and her daughters, which are mostly completely open down the front, it is clearly evident that this was also their custom, and we can be sure that Nefertiti's daughters were brought up to appreciate the elegance that centuries later made Cleopatra turn back to the cosmetic knowledge of the past in ancient Egypt, to discover its secrets for her own use. Occasionally the women at Amarna wore, under their open coat-frocks, a long sheath-like garment apparently ending in tights, as Ankhkhesenamen wears in the Frontispiece. This was presumably for their own convenience and warmth.

One of Petrie's most memorable and skilled recoveries from their home, was the remaining part of the painted wall scene of the King and Queen with their six daughters, as mentioned before. It can be seen from reconstructions of the mural, that Akhenaten was seated on its left (our right) and opposite him was Nefertiti in a seductively languid pose, half reclining on piled up cushions, probably not long after the birth of the sixth princess. The baby sits on her lap; the three eldest girls stand between their parents, encircled by Nefertiti's left arm, necessarily lengthened for the purpose, in the usual way Egyptian artists unselfconsciously overcame any such difficulties. The baby, no longer visible, stretches out her very tiny hand towards her oldest sister who reaches out her arm towards her, and in the Petrie Museum there is a small fragment of painted plaster with the baby's tiny hand on it, proving she was there! Nefertiti's wide, red sash falls from her waist on to cushions on the floor by her side, where the very young, fourth and fifth princesses sit playing and fondling each other. This tender little fragment (Fig. 11) rescued by Petrie (who winkled it off the broken plaster wall, which has been described as a feat of genius) is housed in the Ashmolean Museum, Oxford.

Fig. 11. Mural of princesses in a family group

The painting retains the soft reds, clear blues and yellows. They resemble those so frequently found in the glazed inlays, which must often have been made into pictures of this sort - an earlier form of the mosaic pictures of the Middle Ages in Europe. The two little princesses, Nefernefruaten-the-Younger (her mother's name) and Nefernefru-re (the Aten in this later name was changed into Re) wear bead collars, bracelets and ear-rings, and the toe-nails of their tiny feet are painted white. Their heads are elongated at the back, a convention which in the earlier days of Egyptology was thought by some to show they *all* had water on the brain! This incredible idea is now recognised as not credible, especially as when they are grown up and the art was in its naturalistic period they are shown as perfectly normal, as is Ankhsenamen and Tutankhamen in the Frontispiece. The children are often shown barefooted, and no doubt in the hot summer days were kept cooler by having their hair bundled up at the back of the neck, which would have then shown as a bulge.

The comfortable cushions in this picture are decorated with coloured diamond patterns and there are glazed fragments in the Museum of just such patterns from the cushions, in similar but inlaid scenes, against the usual rich red backgrounds. Further fragments from this mural were found by John Pendlebury; they showed the columns supporting the roof, probably of their smaller sitting room, with blinds drawn over the windows for coolness, and rows of jars of cool drinks, beer and wine for the grown-ups and no doubt fruit juices for the princesses. Pendlebury wrote "no more delightful scene was ever painted; the colours are as fresh as when they were first laid on".

The status of artists at Amarna was high. Palace artists are shown at work on some of the features with which they beautified the buildings. In the tomb of Huya, Queen Ty's administrator, who accompanied her on her visit to the capital, there is a series of scenes recording for all time the outstanding skills of the artists and their training to gain them. Perhaps the scenes were included in the tomb of this vizier as a mark of Huya's immense admiration for the heights they attained, and his astonishment at their new approach. One of these scenes (Fig. 12) shows the actual studio of the chief sculptor, Auta. With a painter's palette in his left hand, he raises a brush in his right hand to put the finishing touches on a statue of Princess Baketaten, who came to Amarna with Queen Ty. She is described as 'King's daughter', possibly of Queen Ty's husband as she is younger than one would expect a child of the Queen-Mother to be by this time. If this were so, she would have been Akhenaten's half-sister. Her statue stands on a raised platform so that her face is opposite Auta's and her youthful figure is fully shown in a wide-open coat, not even tied under the breast as most gowns were. She holds a fruit to her breast.

Auta's head is too big for his body. Was this a real picture shown to perpetuate his likeness? Did he carve this scene himself, or did one of his students? It

(From another scene).

Fig. 12. Studio of the chief sculptor, Auta

reminds one of those Italian Renaissance pictures where sometimes the artist is shown amongst the onlookers in his own picture; or in Spain, where Velasquez painted himself painting. Here Auta is actually named in his own studio.

His apprentices are shown in his workshop starting, as we know so many Italian artists did nearly 3,000 years later, by helping their master and watching his work. One student leans forward so eagerly to watch Auta's technique with a paint brush that he is literally peering at him. "Why she's alive" he exclaims: a tribute to Amarna naturalism! Another in the background is carving a chair leg with a light adze; below him, on a stool, sits another craftsman using a chisel on a bewigged model of a wooden head. Under this, a coarse and fine chisel are shown horizontally suspended in the air *over* the box in which they are kept: not 'weightless' but shown so that they can be visible to the viewer instead of being hidden in the box. These skilled and honoured artists were clearly proud of their tools. The tool box has a recess the shape of the chisels to protect their edges when fitted into it. Above him is the craftsman with the adze, shaping the chair leg with the usual claw foot on a block; and a peg at the top to fit into the hole or mortise in the chair. Below the figure of Auta, another crafts-man is carving a stone column which has the usual palm-leaf capital. Others, from another part of the wall, are pounding stone, making vases and working in metal for such ornaments as the gold collars. The jug and basins from another scene are very like those used in Victorian bedrooms, and even later in English country houses.

Such scenes as these of artists shown at work on all the different types of materials and techniques in the actual palace workshops and studios, give us a feeling of personal contact and insight, more than some of the earlier and very lovely carvings of craftsmen at work. From the Old Kingdom, there are scenes of cobblers, stone-carvers, metal-workers, rope-makers, wine-pressers and as noted, even scent-makers. But here we have a named artist carving a statue of a member of the family, and the busyness of it all brings us nearer to the people themselves. It makes us indebted to Akhenaten and Nefertiti for allowing a mirror to be held so frequently to the details, not only to their own doings, but to the life of the ordinary people around them. It is a piece of historical luck that despite the utter despoliation of the city, it was never overbuilt, and the shadows are there, cast by the pictures of its beautiful past.

Another artistic relic which seems to be special to Amarna, is the series of limestone statuettes of monkeys employed in many of the activities of man. These monkey statuettes are small enough to hold in the hand and are care-lessly finished, as though made for amusement by a craftsman in an idle mom-ent or two; or they might have been toys. In any case, they show an ironic sense of humour. Some of them could be humorous asides about the royal family and the court doings, with monkeys driving a horse and chariot for in-stance, and kissing a young monkey held on their knee - both oft repeated royal scenes. There are 25 of these coloured limestone figurines in the Petrie Museum showing monkeys playing the harp, practising acrobatics, eating and drinking, while some cosset their young in a typically affectionate way. Some mischievous youngsters are busily plundering food from a sack. A number are coloured and shaped on both sides. Pendlebury believed that some were a comment on human behaviour. Certainly a number in the collection suggest the enjoyment of them may have been on two levels: one for amusement; another perhaps, failing news-papers, as cartoons!

46

V The Central City of Amarna

The royal residence, as we have noted, was separate from the central and more official palace, to which it was joined by the famous fly-over bridge. The whole of this royal estate covered more ground than Versailles and Fontainebleau put together - with some to spare. In the palace, the northern 'harem' was obviously a place of privacy for Nefertiti and her daughters, ladies-in-waiting and attendants. The word *harem* is sometimes misunderstood to mean only the section of the palace reserved for the king's concubines, but it means the women's apartments and is used to describe the santuaries of royal women.

Petrie named Nefertiti's apartment, on the side of the palace nearest to (but guarded from) the bridge entrance, 'the Queen's pavilion'. It was one of the most elaborate and beautifully decorated wings of the huge building, smaller, and more regularly planned than the immense, decorated, columned and stately reception halls, leading on from one into another down the centre of the building. He describes the Queen's own room as 'gorgeous', a daringly descriptive and unscientific adjective for the discreet terms usually employed by archaeologists.

The glazed wall tiles, inlaid with figures and flowers, had fallen into the sand from the walls plundered and carried away for the stone. But some, with their lovely colourings are preserved in museums, especially Petrie's own. Lotus garlands shone against a red ground; coloured water reeds, the persea fruit, cornflowers, daisies and minutiae are inlaid, resembling the delicacy of such flowers in the early European mosaics. He brought back thousands of the red clay moulds in which these pieces had been made and then glazed, and he actually managed to preserve one elaborately painted floor until, alas, it was smashed by some workers who resented tourists walking across their fields. He described the floor painting as having a deep blue central pool with fish swimming in it and lotuses spreading over it, while duck, marsh birds, butterflies and dragonflies cross the sky above it. (Fig. 13) Petrie's drawing of it, shows flowering bushes and rows of flowers in vases encircling it, probably just as they were arranged in the houses.

Fig. 13. Fragment of painted palace pavement

Along the pathways of these painted floors, foreign captives were often pictured, although the designs were mainly of plants and animals. The artists showed intense observation and a loving truthfulness. Instead of the more rigid, earlier Egyptian designs, or the formal rosettes and circles of Babylonian patterns, the individuality of the plants was faithfully reproduced; the cool, still outlines of the water lilies contrasting with the waving branches of the tall and more flexible thistles.

In the centre of the pavilion was a columned courtyard with a pool of real water in the middle, about fifteen feet deep. It was covered by a roof raised on finely sculptured pillars, no doubt for shade as well as privacy. The Queen's name and titles were fully set out on the coping of the well. The water was channelled into it from the river at flood times; but Petrie suggests, from his findings at one end of the court, that when the Nile was low, the water from the river was raised into the pool by a chain of buckets operating as some kind of water wheel or *sakkieh*. It would be surprising if the people who made the pyramids, and had wheel-made pottery as long ago as that, did not find some wheel-method to raise the water from the Nile. At Amarna they made artificial lakes in the desert, in the central city, and at the North and South Palaces, and it seems unlikely that they would have waited for the very much later invention of the Greek water-screw to help them fill these large lakes. There were dados of modelled ducks carved below the capitals of the columns, and bands carved around the columns with scenes of the royal family. Many of these coloured tiles can be seen in the Petrie Museum.

Behind the rows of columns were small rooms with low, thin, overlapping screen walls just inside the entrances for privacy, which was further ensured by hanging bead curtains, for which a place had been provided. At the back of these cubicles, there were brick recesses for a bed six feet long (approx. 2 metres) and two feet wide, with other benches for seats and personal equipment. These cubicles would have enabled a restful siesta in the middle of the day. But not all was silent or serious in these beautiful surroundings. There are carved harem scenes showing the well-known musical formation of a women's quartet, with one playing a harp, two plucking lutes and a fourth a lyre, while a fifth girl claps her hands and dances gaily to the music.

Amongst the many thousands of red clay moulds in which the various designs were made, the 'palmette' shape was a favourite one, shown variously as a palm leaf, or radiating petals, or a pointed tree, with varied details. One variation is very like those on the handles of a bronze dish in the treasure of Vix, that collection of objects from about a thousand years after Amarna, which was discovered in the 1950s near the source of the Seine, and is now in the Museum of Chatillon-sur-Seine. Had the palmette design on these handles made

its way through Greece, into Italy and over the Alps into northern France, from ancient Egypt or further east? In the Vix collection found in France, for instance, the magnificent bronze vase which stands over five feet high (1.52 metres) is decorated with attached, but rounded models of horses, lions, snakes and figurines in which

AMARNA   VIX

Fig. 14. Palmette designs

elements of Greek, Etruscan, Cretan and oriental art can be seen. In some of the fine pairs of horses around the frieze the head of the outside horse is shown facing the viewer instead of in profile. This is parallel with Amarna relief carvings, some of which are in the royal tomb, where the outside horse turns to face the viewer. (Fig. 15) The charm' of the Amarna reliefs is in their naive vitality; they are without the sophistication of the bronze horses, but the idea of the horse turning its face to the viewers is very early, even for ancient Egypt; certainly centuries before the vase.

Fig. 15. Carving of full-faced horse

Outside the palace and at rightangles to it on the north side was the Great Aten Temple with its huge front towers or gateway pylons facing the river. The next largest Aten temple was the Chapel Royal beside the royal residence, with a private entrance for the family across from their home, although it fronted the royal road, just past the Bridge. The pylon-gateways flanking the entrance to the temples were slotted with niches for tall flag poles; and more pylons led to its inner courts. Always and everywhere these buildings were roofless - open to the sun from every angle - and the sculptors carving the reliefs of the King and Queen at worship, cleverly met this new dimension by carving the reliefs at different angles so that the light at all times of the day gave emphasis to the proceedings. This they did by varying the carving techniques, using high and low relief even in the one figure, (Pl. V) so that wherever the sun was, it illuminated the Aten scene by light and shadows, at all times of the day; even the desert moonlight was thus effective. This was in complete contrast to their work formerly carved in roofed temples or at best in the shaded courtyards. But they met this adventure of change to emphasise their meaning - just one of the innovations in Amarna art. Besides using the direct light and deep shadows so skilfully, they gradually learnt to represent royalty as they saw them in real life - letting them age, and express emotion, eventually attaining a naturalism of excellence.

The other buildings in the central city, the outlines of which can still be discerned in the sand, include the Priest's Quarters, the Store Houses, and a sacred lake. There was also 'The Place of Correspondence of the Pharaoh', which we might call the Record or Foreign Office today. There the official correspondence between Egypt and the Eastern countries was kept. Stored on shelves were hundreds of little blocks of dried mud-bricks inscribed in the cuneiform script - the diplomatic form used in a variety of languages of the time. This is written with a wedge-shaped stilo pressed into damp clay, leaving what looks to those who cannot read it like a series of higgledy-piggledy lines, described by one writer as though a small bird had hopped about on the damp clay leaving its little claw marks all over it. In these 'Amarna Letters' we could have had a full history of the advance of the Hittites on the smaller states in the Near and Middle East, but the peasants used the dried mud-brick as compost, and when some of them tried to save these little blocks, they hawked them about in sacks, unrecognised, until many were reduced to the dust from which they came, leaving our knowledge very patchy. What a historical loss! It was once thought that Akhenaten, in his pursuit of the Aten, ignored foreign affairs, but it is now considered that the policy of keeping a balance of power amongst the great powers in the Near East was continued in his reign. It is known that he instigated military action to suppress Bedouin in Nubia, and continued his father's policy of temple and town building as far up the river as the third and fourth Cataract. We know Amarna had a 'University', or 'House of Life' where young scribes were taught writing: and further to the east the barracks, from which the soldiery patrolled the high desert, where their tracks are still visible today from when they guarded the city against bandits and robbers. Nothing is new!

The mud-brick houses belonging to the courtiers, clerks and workers, intermingled in the various streets off the main 'royal' highway. Many rooms were

Plate V. Nefertiti offering showing variations in low
            and high relief carving

decorated with friezes of fruit, flowers, or formal patterns painted on white-washed walls. Where carpets were used, skins, woven rugs or rope mats served the purpose and sometimes embroidered textiles were thrown over couches and chairs. Beds are shown in some of the Amarna carvings, mounted on beautifully carved legs with lions' paws for feet, lifted on turned blocks, as on Tutankh-amen's throne. One bed is shown with a well padded mattress (drawn on its side so it can be fully seen!) being held in place by the footboard at the lower end of the bed, although the head-rest is perched rather precariously on the slope at the top. On a base of board or plaited wicker, the fat, soft-looking mattress would be filled with feathers and covered with linen. One such bed on a platform, is so high on its mounted legs that it had to be reached by three steps beside it - rather like a mounting block for getting on a horse. Was this, one wonders, because of a fear of snakes and scorpions? Around the bed were tables with delicacies to eat and drink, and jewellery put out ready to wear the next day. Scented cosmetics for toilet use were part of the equipment.

When John Pendlebury was excavating in 1936 his team were living in the north 'dig' house. It was called by the press the oldest house in the world because its walls were built literally on those left from an Amarna house of about 1370 B.C. The stone bases from the columns were still there, although the painted, wooden columns had long since been eaten by the white ants. This 'dig' house in which we were living was some miles from the excavations and we used to leave about 3 a.m. in the cold of a desert morning which only those who have experienced it can believe. Wrapped in woollies over summer clothes for later in the day, when the "Aten would fill every land with its beauty", and hoping not to tread on a scorpion sleeping just below the top-sand, we would mount our donkeys and ride to the excavation under the high, ink-blue night sky, lit by the brightness of the stars. As we rode, the delicate flush of the early dawn crept from the East and began to spread, touching the high cliffs with its cool light until the colours warmed and intensified as the sun rose and flooded the plain with its life-giving light, making great sense of Akhenaten's poem of praise to it as 'the Aten'. Off would come our woollies and as we reached the 'dig', on would go the sun-glasses as we dismounted to see the work in progress.

One particular morning John Pendlebury called us over to see the excavators uncovering, layer by layer, something brightly coloured lying on the sand. It was one half of the painted double door of a house, decorated with the bright yellow, painted rays of the sun streaming down on to where the King and Queen had been shown standing to worship it. The wood of the door had long since perished; what lay on the sand was but a layer of paint. Had there been a desert breeze it would have blown away as the sand itself, but there was no wind and photography was able to capture the beauty of the door of this house through which an ordinary Amarna family must have gone in and out so long ago, possibly banging it at times.

The average private house had a main living room in the centre with the other rooms built around it, which kept it cool. The central room was not dark, however, as its walls were higher than the surrounding ones and there were 'clerestory' windows at the top, above the height of the rest of the roof. Some put those roofs to good use, as a loggia for sitting out in the cool of the evenings. Although built of mud brick, the better houses were mounted on clay

52

bricks, and the more important the owner, the more clay bricks there were. Another distinctive feature was that the door jambs were made of stone and had a stone lintel across the top. This had the names and titles of the house-owner carved on it - an easier way to guide the seeker than the names and numbers of some London streets! The walls were thick for coolness with at least the front one often whitewashed.

As mentioned, the bathrooms in the bigger houses had stone 'splash' walls behind the bath. One small stone seat was found in its former place beside where the bath had been, and on it, there were still the little bowls for cosmetics, with grease in one and some crystals in another. Despite this sophistication, the drainage was elementary. Beside the lavatory, were two compartments for sand, with dippers in them for scooping it out, but the limestone lavatory seat, supported on bricks, was comfortably shaped.

Servants' quarters and the kitchens themselves were mostly built separately, and on the east side of the house, out of the path of the prevailing wind which could bring the fumes of the cooking oil and the smell of onions to the house. The bread was baked in pottery moulds in ovens of baked clay bricks. The bakery benches were at a convenient height for kneading the dough on them, the flour having been made in the age-old way of grinding the corn on stone. Large bins for storing quantities of grain were shaped like bee-hives and were built outside houses. But ordinary store cupboards were built in the houses and effective cellarettes were made in sunken brick-lined hollows in the ground. Some dog kennels were found; and it would seem there were family cats also kept as pets. They ate the mice who ate the grain; and there was of course the great cat goddess Bast. But so many figures of cats of all shapes and sizes and cat families with the kittens round their mother were made, in the popular glazed faience, that it would seem they must have been loved as pets, as well as being kept for their practical and religious purposes. Where horses were kept for a chariot, or in the barracks for riding, they had cobbled floors with a tethering stone. Some of the watering troughs for them were of alabaster, and there is one in the British Museum, from the Northern Palace, which is carved around the sides with peacefully grazing deer.

Pleated kilts were made for men in woven linen cloth, and long dresses and pleated capes for women. For ordinary wear, both men and women often wore a plainer robe reaching down the leg. The priests were not the only people with shaven heads; men and women would have felt much cooler and cleaner under the wigs they wore. The wide bead collarettes, like the one worn by Nefertiti in Plate I, were worn by both men and women, especially when they are shown in scenes of luxurious banquets. These banquet scenes were painted on tomb walls in the XVIIIth Dynasty showing bewigged and elegantly gowned men and women sitting together enjoying the luxuries. Girls in 'bikini-wear' danced for them and handed them delicacies and lotuses, in great contrast to the record we have of the comparatively simple, family feast in the palace at Amarna, with the children present. (Fig. 27)

In the earlier carvings of Ramose's tomb in Thebes, he is shown giving one of the more elaborate dinner parties, with his pretty wife beside him as together they entertain their family and friends. Wives are shown fully enjoying all the sensuous delicacies and food and drink with their husbands, quite unlike the later Greek wives who seemed so often to have been left at home - spinning. Ramose's father and beautiful mother are shown at his dinner party; and his brother, with his wife May, who has one arm affectionately round their daughter's shoulders. Beneath May's chair, though obviously un-beknown to her, is an observantly carved detail of a cat with one paw stretched out towards a small bird who, with open beak, has been captured by the artist in a moment of terror, but also of action as its wings are widespread to rise and escape the predatory paw. Perhaps they were both after the crumbs. The surrounding carvings with displays of food, and the servants and offering bearers, are exquisitely carved to show the refinements and pleasures of the banquet.

The wigs and gowns worn by the guests are so elegantly detailed in the fine stone that they could serve as fashion plates for XVIIIth Dynasty styles. A friend is shown at the banquet with his wife Merel, who sits languidly and elegantly beside her husband, with one arm around his shoulders. Her long curled wig hangs just below her shoulders and her deep collar-necklace must have had hundreds of beads in it - lapis lazuli and carnelian as well as glazed forms. Beneath it, her robe is drawn together just below her breast. She wears no undergarment and her thighs are visible under the sheer diaphanous linen of the gown, despite its pleats which swirl around her small feet.

Women moved freely and enjoyably about their world, socially and at work, with no sign of being inhibited. Many examples of the beads from colourful collars like Nefertiti's on Plate I are in the Petrie Museum, with one collar reconstructed from the actual beads found. Wide bracelets were popular too, and although Nefertiti's were probably of gold and silver, and stolen long ago, there are, in the Museum, some fragments made of vibrant sky-blue, glazed faience, varying from about a centimetre wide to two inches (5 cm.). These one can see in the Museum, with the charms and amulets. Some have the circles remaining from when they had dangled from jewellery; and some glazed flowers still have the threading-holes through them for sewing on dresses and capes. One can safely assume from the number of rings found (and the number of moulds in which they were made), varying from plain bands, to rings with gods and goddesses or lucky symbols engraved on them, and even in the cases of royalty, metal ones with the names of the owner, that absolutely everyone must have worn them.

VI   Life at Amarna

Most of the scenes left to us of Akhenaten's and Nefertiti's active partnership at Amarna come from the decorated walls in the rock tombs of the statesmen, high up in the cliffs. One of the most delightful is a family scene from the tomb of the leading nobleman Ay. It is in complete contrast to that in the tomb of Ramose in Thebes, where none of the royal children is present and Nefertiti is shown standing demurely behind the King. Davies, who copied all the tomb scenes, speaks of the size and beauty of Ay's tomb, and wrote that it was comparatively free from bats. This last comment interests us less than it did him, when he sat for weeks on end copying the wonderful pictures, for here is NefernefruatenNefertiti taking part in regal affairs. This is no goddess with the King, but his regal partner participating in a manner not known before in a State occasion.

The carving was never finished and neither the King's robes nor hers had yet been added, but their unmistakable blue crowns and the Aten's blessing hands on them were obviously put in first, as can be seen in Figure 16. Nefertiti, no longer a passive follower, is actually handing over the treasured Gold Collars, making the recipients 'People of Gold', just as our own reigning Queen awards the British Honours to the people who have won them. The three eldest children are with their parents. Meritaten the eldest and Maketaten the second daughter are helping their mother, possibly as a distraction to keep them quiet through the ceremony, as well as teaching them royal duties. The third princess, Ankhesenpa-aten (Ankh-es-en-pa-aten) is too young yet for such responsibilities, although she is the only one of the three, whom we know became a Queen of Egypt - as Tutankhamen's wife. In this scene, Meritaten has a collar in her left hand ready to give to Nefertiti, and two others on a tray balanced on her right hand. Maketaten, steadies herself by an arm around her mother's neck, while very unsteadily she wobbles another gold collar *off* the tray in her other hand.

Below the window, receiving the Gold Collars is Ay, 'Overseer of His Majesty's Horses' as well as 'Father of the God': and *most* remarkably, also his

Fig. 16. Unfinished scene of Nefertiti awarding Gold Collars to the nobleman Ay, and his wife Tey. The princesses are trying to help

wife Tey, because it is otherwise unknown for women to be included in such a
ceremony. Other gifts are piled up beside them; metal vases; fillets to wear
round the head; necklaces, and red *gloves* for Ay, perhaps for his horsemanship.
They were probably made of dyed leather, and are a very early picture, if not
the first, of gloves in ancient Egypt. In the next scene, Ay is leaving the palace
wearing the precious gloves which he holds out for the admiration of his welcoming friends, who are actually touching them almost in disbelief at his gift.
(Fig. 17)

Fig. 17. Ay being hailed by his friends as he leaves the palace with his honours and awards

The German Egyptologist Borchardt, who unearthed the Berlin portrait
of Nefertiti, asked earlier in this century if Ay's title 'Father of the God' could
mean Father of the Queen? It has never been known in what relation Tey stood
to the Queen, but her title 'The Nurse who Fostered the Divine' has been taken
by some to mean she was the nursing mother of Nefertiti and breast-fed her

when she was a baby. This cannot be proved. But there are some remarkably relevant features. For instance, the suckling of grown pharaohs by goddesses, sometimes in strange guises, was a recognised ritual. Rameses II is shown being suckled by the goddess Isis and in another scene where he stands in warrior-like pose holding the warlike weapon of a mounted mace-head, he is accepting the breast of the goddess Anukis of the Aswan region. There is also the picture

of Hathor in the form of a sycamore tree suckling King Tuthmosis III. (Fig. 18) Tey was not a goddess. She was apparently the real-life wife of Ay. But Madame Desroches-Noblecourt has described a scene on a block in the Louvre, which may link the underlying significance of these scenes of goddesses nourishing pharaohs, with Tey and Nefertiti. On the right of the Louvre carving is the upper left side of a women's body once described as the *King*. But the shape of her long heavy breast, which is carved in great detail with a fulsome nipple, is unimaginable on even a fat man with a grossly developed chest. It is a hanging full breast formed by the glands of a woman; and this woman wears a Gold Collar. As Madame Desroches-Noblecourt has pointed out we know of no other woman but Tey who received this masculine honour. The woman's left hand, carved with typical Amarna length and flexibility, is offering her

Fig. 18. Tuthmosis III being suckled by the goddess Hathor in her form of a sycamore tree. (From the King's tomb, Thebes)

breast (in the ritual gesture of offering to a king), to the very fragmentary figure of a slim young girl on the left of the carving, who is stretching out her right arm towards the older woman. The block from above this one, on which the head of each woman was carved, is missing. But could this young feminine figure be the youthful Nefertiti with Tey, in a scene reminiscent of the suckling of kings? Madame Desroches-Noblecourt's suggestion cannot be discounted. As well as Tey being 'Great Nurse' to the Queen, her titles include 'Handmaid to the King' and 'True of Voice', a verification of moral excellence. Her status seems almost to equal that of Ay.

58

On the wall showing Ay leaving the palace and being greeted by his friends, it can be seen in Figure 17 that a part of it, in the centre, is encircled by a line. When Davies came to copy this wall, the ringed area faced him as a gaping hole. The friends were no longer there. He had to copy this part of the scene from a drawing made by early scholars in the nineteenth century, before the tomb robbers had hacked it from the wall. When Petrie was excavating later in the nineteenth century he found in the city, near the site of the artists' studios, a squared block of stone with the unfinished figure on it of a humble little man rejoicing. Being so near the sculptors' workshops he thought it was probably an unfinished student's trial-piece and brought it back. But in fact it is the last unfinished figure in that scene, at the back of the group, wearing an ordinary wig, a pubic sheath and raising his head and arms in welcome to his master. He could well have been one of Ay's horsemen, as his dress is that of grooms, sentries, charioteers and the soldiery. It is not a fine piece of carving and was probably selected to steal because of its unrecognisability as part of a crowd scene. The tomb robbers must have hacked it from the wall to sell, but dropped it as they hurried across the plain with other stolen loot, perhaps even to a waiting boat to carry them to a market. It was not an artist's trial piece, and some years ago it was recognised by the writer in the Petrie Museum as being from Ay's tomb. Such are the adventures in Museums - the sort of 'find' that gives the thrill of a rescue on the site of a dig.

The window scene is a popular illustration in the tombs, and the one in that of Parennefer's is finished and delicately coloured, perhaps because he was Akhenaten's head craftsman and chose to show to advantage the skills of his workmen in his own memorial. The pleated robes of the King and Queen are very similar in design except that the top of the King's hip-wrap can be seen. Both wear thin bracelets on their upper arms and wide armlets, probably of gold, inscribed with plaques of the Aten's two names. Akhenaten also has some of these plaques (of which there are some faience examples in the Petrie Museum) suspended from his wide bead collar. The Aten welcomes Nefertiti with a hand around her waist and one on her breast. The King waves to Parennefer and Nefertiti leans forward on a cushioned window sill in a greeting to him. The cushion is designed with the diamond pattern, like the cushions on which the two little princesses were plumped at the feet of their parents, in the mural from their home, now in the Ashmolean Museum, Oxford. The children are not shown in the window, but are never far away: in this scene they are shown in an adjoining room, perhaps an ante-room, with their taller and dignified aunt, Nefertiti's sister Benretmut. (Fig. 19)

A variation of a window as a place from which to give royal awards, is shown in a tomb where the King and Queen are receiving Meryra near a quayside. In the building, Meryra is pictured as laden with gold collars, the result of

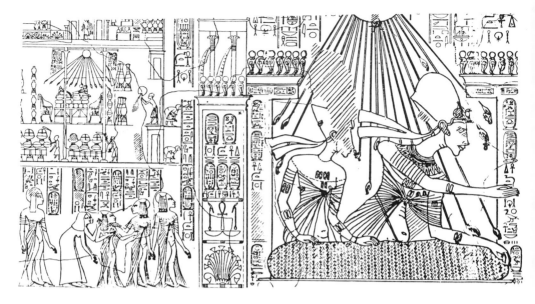

Fig. 19. The Royal Family at a State occasion

services rendered. In his office, as High Priest of the Aten, he was responsible for superintending the store houses, particularly for the offerings on the altars of the Aten; and further along the wall is a scene on the banks of the river, where the tribute has arrived in boats. Thirteen of them are moored side by side with their masts making an interlaced pattern - a veritable forest of rigging as sailing boats have when close together. The captain and the crew are on deck, bowing to the waist, and at this double ceremony of an Investiture and an Inspection, Nefertiti wears the 'cap' crown of kings. (Fig. 20)

In the scenes of worship of the Aten, the royal partnership is undeniably and unmistakably complete: their roles interchangeable - their rituals identical. At Amarna they are shown everywhere together, whereas in Thebes, Nefertiti's independence was stressed, possibly to mark her status as Queen Regnant, now accepted without surprise. Sometimes standing on opposite sides of an altar, they offer to the god the same tributes, or vary them, one giving flowers and the other censing, or pouring libations, or one or both upholding the *Sekhem* sceptre showing the recognition of their equal authority. Often they are shown side by side, but with Nefertiti carved as following the King so that her ritual can be seen by the viewer. Otherwise, as when they are actually side by side at the high altar, little more of Nefertiti shows beyond the King than her full flowing skirt, her ceremonial action to the god being obscured, although they stand in the same relationship to the god they worship.

60

Nefertiti also performed the ritual of 'Purification' in libation ceremonies to the god, which were normally the act only of the King or Priest. In vessels of gold, silver, bronze and of glazed pottery, sometimes with a spout shaped as the feather of Maat, the goddess of truth, Nefertiti's performance of this religious function is emphasised by the special attention paid to the carving. As can be seen in the Petrie Museum in such scenes (Pl. V), the Queen's long flexible hands and the vessel she offers are carved in a variety of techniques, combining high and low carving in raised and sunken relief, so that wherever the sun shone the scene would be accentuated by bright light and deep shade. This was taken full advantage of in the Aten temples which were open to the direct light of the sky.

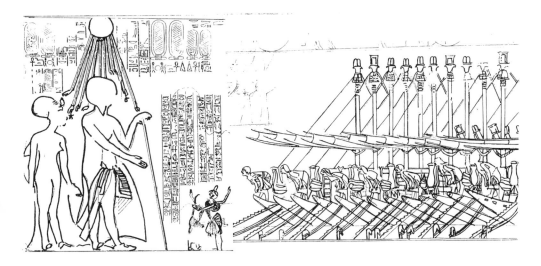

Fig. 20. The monarchs at Meryra's investiture and the inspection of boats

In one such scene, the rays of the Aten are straight-sided and deeply cut, throwing a dark shadow to join the Queen with the god, one of whose rays passes protectively behind her in telling perspective. Both Akhenaten and Nefertiti are shown together wearing the *Atef* kings' crown at such ceremonies. It is a large and heavy crown mounted on ram's horns and the Queen's is slightly simplified like the one the boy-king Tutankhamen wears (see Frontispiece).

In the tomb of Apy, their offering is that of the two names of the Aten in ornamented double cartouches on stands, probably of gold or silver. On the King's offering are images of *Shu*, the god of the air, wearing his triple feathers on his head, just as Nefertiti does in another scene. But the remarkable thing is, and it *is* remarkable, that while the Aten's names in the King's offering face the Aten, which would be expected - in Nefertiti's offering, the god's names *still face her, and her image*. Some deep metaphysical meaning seems to underlie this reversal of the name of the god Aten to face Nefertiti. Nowhere else in Egyptian history is the name of a god constantly reversed to face even a king. Whereas Akhenaten was the royal son and heir to the throne, and possibly Nefertiti was not even of royal blood, Akhenaten may have felt this unprecedented honour paid to her was visual evidence of her 'divine' regality. So extraordinary was this fact of writing a god's name back to front in an inscription, that early Egyptologists, if they noticed it, possibly judged it as a mistake.

Hieroglyphs are written to be read *either* from the left *or* from the right, with all the living things - people, birds, beasts, even plants, facing the beginning of the inscription. But in Nefertiti's full name the reed ($\big\}$) in the Aten's name at the top of her cartouche is always reversed to face her image below it. Whichever way the thousands of inscriptions are written, the name of the god Aten ( ) always faces Nefertiti. In 1973 Dr. Wilson of Chicago, recognising this honour to Nefertiti in all the carvings of her full name, drew attention to its significance. "The reversed writing," he noted, "is so unusual that it stands out in the texts with an emphasis like capital letters in modern writing . . even her gifted husband did not enjoy this eye-catching relation to the god."

In the tomb of Apy, Nefertiti's description is:

> "Hereditary Princess, great in favour,
> Lady of Grace, given gladness,
> The Aten rises to shed favour on her
> And sets to multiply her love.
> The Great and Beloved Wife of the King
> Mistress of South and North
> Lady of Two Lands: may she live forever."

At Amarna, Akhenaten and Nefertiti shared the godliness of a pharaoh in the prayers of the nobles who 'worship' and 'adore' them and the Aten equally, using these reverent forms of address employed for a god or pharaoh. They and the Aten, are all asked equally for the same overwhelming desire of all ancient Egyptians - eternal life, a proper burial, continuous offerings after 'death' and the call of their names to ensure their continuity. This is the true worship for a god, and two Kings of equally god-like powers.

But life at Amarna was not all State and religious duties. The family ranged far and wide over the plain in their chariots, particularly north and south where they had small palaces. These were beautiful buildings and evidently 'retreats', as the lay-outs of both suggest they were designed for holidays. The few miles between the town centre and each of these palaces could have been sailed by river, but journeys were apparently also made by chariot as there are many scenes of the King and Queen driving along together, *and* separately, for Nefertiti is shown driving her own chariot in kingly fashion. One wonders what Queen Ty thought of the expertise of her daughter-in-law managing her own horses and the flimsy chariot. Many have mocked at the idea of Nefertiti, regal Queen of Egypt driving her own chariot, but she was far from being a stereotyped royal wife or woman pharaoh. Those of us who learnt to manage horses when we were young are not amazed; nor at the princesses who are shown driving their own small chariots. The manageability of intelligent and well trained

Fig. 21. The King and Queen share the *Ankh* of life while Meritaten goads the horse

63

horses is within the scope of someone taught how to handle them; and with Ay as 'Overseer of the King's Horses', Nefertiti and the princesses would have had the same opportunities as Akhenaten to learn horsemanship and chariot driving from the most skilled horsemen of the day, and with the best horses in the royal stables at their disposal.

Many royal figures have been experts with horses. As for the Amarna princesses shown as handling the sagacious animals, it is perhaps more surprising to read that in Victorian England, our Regnant Queen Victoria's daughter, Princess Helena was, in her childhood, allowed by Prince Albert, the Prince Consort, to *groom* her own mare. Whether or not equestrian lessons went that far at Amarna is not known. But there is no reason why Nefertiti should not have driven her own chariot in the style of a king, as she is repeatedly carved as doing in their 'expedition' scenes; nor why the growing girls, who appear reasonably sturdy, young people, should not have had the joy of being taught to handle their horses. Nefertiti was, perhaps, safer driving her own chariot than as pictured in the tomb of Mahu, the Chief of Police, where Akhenaten is driving them both in his vehicle. (Fig. 21) He has the reins in his right hand, but rather perilously, his back is turned to the horses as he faces Nefertiti and shares with her the only *one* Ankh of Life which is being handed to them both by the Aten. This protective symbol may have brought them luck as the young Meritaten is leaning mischievously forward in front of the chariot with a stick to prod the rump of the plumed and spirited animals.

In the tomb of Panehesy, the King drives his own chariot (the back wheel of it can be seen in Figure 22). Here, without his beloved Nefertiti to turn to, he faces his horses. Nefertiti is shown as though behind him, but being carved higher up, the picture really conveys that she is further away, showing the viewer of the scene that she is on the far side of the King *beside* him. Wearing her dignified tall crown, she holds the reins expertly in her right hand with a proper regard for her pair of horses, which she is observantly driving at a gallop. In her left hand, she rather nonchalantly holds a whip behind her. The sheathed arrow case on her chariot is kings' equipment, but as noted before, there are no scenes of royal hunts in this reign as are shown in others, and apparently even Akhenaten did not go to war, despite peace-keeping conflicts in Nubia and possibly the Near East. A military escort went ahead of the royal chariots and behind, at the end of the royal procession, came the police of which Mahu was the Chief. Even in those days, officials were engaged in security arrangements.

Another scene shows the princesses driving their own horses and chariot. They are just setting off (and perhaps showing off?) as their large retinue of ladies-in-waiting are being driven by grooms. Evidently Nefertiti was satisfied with the arrangements, as in this tomb it is inscribed that "when she says anything it is done", a description used of the monarch Queen Hatshepsut who ruled earlier in the dynasty. Some of these expeditions were certainly along the 'King's Highway', leading either southward for a sojourn in the cool and beautiful Southern Palace, or northward to the small palace in the northern city.

The design and decoration of this northern building is unique in the ancient world, wrote Pendlebury. It was shown as a centre for nature lovers

Fig. 22. Nefertiti driving her own chariot with the princesses below

with a lake in the central court for birds to swoop happily about, and in another court a colonnaded garden where there appears to have been an aviary. The King would enjoy watching the antics of the birds from a corridor in his suite, which led south to the Queen's suite. But the phenomenal feature of the building was the oblong 'green' room with the four walls entirely covered by a continuous picture of life in the marshes. It was painted so that sitting, or even standing in the room (because the murals reached some 10 feet high), one must have felt surrounded by the coolness and privacy of being deep in the shady papyrus marshes and lotus lands around the river. No humans are pictured. No one hunts the birds with a throw-stick or traps them, or harpoons the fish as in the other marsh scenes. Small birds nest in peace and fly over the shimmering waters, with the surface broken only by the zig-zag of the darker blue water sign and the ivory flowers of the open lotuses with their emerald buds and flat green leaves. The river banks are shown in the deep dark of wet mud, contrasting with the delicate tracery of the painted weeds and grasses, and the little gems of their coloured flowers, are as enthralling as any detail in the mosaics of the 4th century A.D.; or the wayside flowers in Botticelli's *Primavera,* or woven into the tapestry of *La Dame à la Licorne.*

The background repetition of tall green stems, making a veritable pallisade of high, straight papyrus growing from their brownish-pink basal leaves, is broken by the nodding of some of their feathery heads across the pattern, and by other stems bending under the weight of a perching bird. Small birds, duck, rock-pigeon and palm-doves enjoy their hide-out; the shrike, with its cruel-shaped beak turns its head about, but has to be satisfied with vine leaves or olives as they hang ripening from the stems amongst the soft green of their leaves. The only break in the rich colourings of the wall scenes was a small door and a long, low window in the end wall, which had a view of the water-garden beyond it.

In the room, the floor and probably the ceiling were white, as a foil to the colouring of the marshes in between, whereas above these scenes water-fowl were probably painted to fly against the white. That part of the frescoes has gone but miraculously, enough of the painted plaster from this unique room was found to piece it together, enabling the scene to be reconstructed. Its transformation from the *typical* marsh scene of Egyptian art, to an inspired, non-functional creation, has been described as approaching the culmination of the artistic peak reached in this remarkable age. All the other marsh scenes have hunting of one sort or another as their *raison d'être,* while the mood evoked by these paintings is one of unutterable peace.

When the family set out in their chariots for the Southern Palace, they would have been anticipating more active enjoyment in a sort of pleasure centre. They could not have known as they entered the dignified, columned halls, that from inscriptions in them, one of the greatest misinterpretations of their history was to occur: and that later, but not until the 1970's, one of the most fundamental clues was to be discovered which would put it right.

Wine jars in the Harem were labelled on their seals with 'The Southern Pool', and as the family left the halls they would see at once the great pool which was really a lake over 120 yards long and half as wide, which sparkled in the sun. It was large enough for the children to skim over it in small pleasure craft, and shallow enough (3 feet) not to be of too much danger if they capsized. This lake in the desert was surrounded by trees and gardens and Leonard Woolley mused, when excavating it, that he found beneath a few centimetres of the desert sand the marks of the trees and the mud borders of the flower beds, with impressions of the stalks and leaves of the once flourishing lotuses and papyrus plants, while time and the plunder for their stone, had completely destroyed the buildings.

Inside the palace there had been covered pools in a roofed hall. Paths circled the pools, with slim columns supporting the roof making a pattern between them. This would have been a cool sanctuary in the heat of the day. Surrounding these indoor pools, at floor level, were vertical walls over a foot high. Did Nefertiti ask for this security to prevent the infants from falling in? *Inside* the pools, whitewashed walls sloped into the water; they were decorated with paintings of flowers rising from a dark painted stripe imitating Nile mud, as though the vegetation were real and growing from the water. There were trellises painted with vines wound around them and clusters of luscious purple grapes hanging from them. The same skilled architectural painters who decorated the North Palace must have been at work here too. The designs were so originally placed.

But it was the pictures made by the coloured inlays in this palace that must have brought visitors to an absolute standstill. Despite the difference in size, the techniques used on the back of Tutankhamen's golden throne (see Frontispiece), give in miniature, an idea of the effect that the walls must have had. Petrie found glazed pieces from the inlays of the royal family, their faces and figures, detailed clothing and crowns of life size, and all inlaid separately as are the figures, clothes and details of Tutankhamen's throne in the Frontispiece. The discs of the sun, which we can be sure, shone over the scenes, were made in blue or red gleaming glaze and were some 8 inches (20 cm.) wide, giving an idea of the scale of some of the inlaid wall scenes.

The technique was different from the mosaic inlays of small fragments, because the pieces were of a whole face, the ear, crown, or clothing worn, and were shaped as such for setting into the wall. Only the furnishing, like the cushions seem to have been constructed of small slim rods, to give a massed multi-coloured effect. No inlays remained in place, but the fallen pieces tell of their beauty. The modelling of the faces was shaped, so as to bring them to life by the play of light and shadow over them. The heads were prepared for crowns to be added in another colour; eyes were inlaid as in Nefertiti's portrait; the eyebrows were separately shaped in curved glass rods; the face and limbs made of red jasper. The total effect of the regalia and environment, in gold and silver and coloured stone and glazes was similar to those used on the back of Tutankhamen's throne, but some were life size and the total effect must have been breathtaking.

During the excavation of this pleasure palace, a misunderstanding arose over the inscriptions some sixty years ago, which created complete confusion in the history of this period up until 1974. It is not surprising that this happened; it was not in the misreading of the hieroglyphs themselves, but *in what lay underneath* them! The clue was literally hidden under the name of Meritaten, which was carved *over* another name which had been hacked out from the stone underneath. This overcarving was first interpreted as meaning that the eldest daughter had supplanted her mother, whose majestic name was thought to have been erased. It strengthened the earlier *theory* that Nefertiti had 'disappeared', and been replaced by a youth, whom it was suggested was Meritaten's husband. Having proceeded along this wrong path, the evidence was not complete enough at that time to correct the error, although we know now, that there is not a scrap of evidence to prove the 'youth' existed.

Leonard Woolley (later Sir Leonard of Ur fame) using his archaeological intelligence and trying to interpret the spirit of the period he was excavating, wrote of the theory that Nefertiti's name was replaced:

> "But Nefertiti if alive could hardly have agreed to so
> public an affront, nor would her death have been
> seized by so devoted a husband as an occasion to
> obliterate her memorials."

Woolley was right. Professor John Harris discovered the mistake. He re-examined many of the overcarvings and the scrapings on the stone *underneath*, left from the former name, and in 1974 he published the fact that the name underneath *was not Nefertiti's*. It was somebody called Kiya. Nobody in the 1920s knew that a woman named Kiya existed. Indeed 50 years later, Professor John Harris only knew of six definite instances of the name of Kiya being used in the Amarna context. One lay undetected in the Petrie Museum. He wrote that not only in the Southern Palace, but in every case where the original name was overcarved but discernible, it was Kiya. The writer, having now seen some of these fragmentary overcarvings from the South Palace fully appreciates the difficulty of discerning the erasures beneath them. But the hieroglyphs left underneath are certainly part of Kiya's name, or her title: not part of Nefertiti's . Conversely, Harris wrote, there is no positive evidence for the overcarving or alteration of *any* inscription of Nefertiti. This left nothing to support the idea of her 'disappearance'. Now we know that Kiya was a secondary wife of Akhenaten's, a harem wife but never his 'Great Royal Wife'.

Kiya's name is never in a royal cartouche; she did not wear the uraeus on the rather distinctive wigs in carvings on the Hermopolis blocks now assessed as being her (whereas the uraeus is essential for the 'Great Royal Wife', *viz.,* Nefertiti); and there is no identifiable evidence of Kiya wearing a crown. Nevertheless, she was Akhenaten's wife, as Harris has pointed out from inscriptions, in the years when she could have borne him two more daughters, and a son, Tutankhamen. If this were so, it would have ensured for Kiya a particular status, and she evidently had apartments at least in the North and South Palaces. But why was her name erased and overcarved? Was there a faction trying to place her in the royal line which would have threatened the legitimate inheritance of the princesses? - or was there an attempt to show that her children were in the direct royal line? On blocks found at Hermopolis Kiya's name is overcarved by those of the princesses Meritaten and Ankhesenpa-aten, as though the children were born to the princesses by their father and not to Kiya.

As Professor Harris has warned us, to construe the erasures of Kiya's name as a fall from grace would be to risk the mistake now evident in the former romantic approach that Nefertiti was 'disgraced'! Kiya may have died. Certainly neither Nefertiti's presence, nor her eminence, was in the least affected by the advent of Akhenaten's secondary wife. But there was an evident need to widen the family. Six princesses, but no prince to make the conventional 'marriage' with his sister the 'heiress', to stabilise the legitimate line on the throne. Nefertiti may not have been able to have had any more children; and with her constantly shown love for her daughters, she would have been anxious for their future. With her intelligence she must have been aware of the need to strengthen the Egyptian throne.

The growing power of the Hittites (who were spreading southwards in the Near East) was increasing in strength, and this threat to the countries in the Near East, to which Egypt was very near, is vividly described in the Amarna Letters. The Kings of the States which were under Egypt's influence - the countries we know of as Syria, the Lebanon, and Israel, with the towns of Byblos, Sidon and Tyre (then ancient Phoenicia), were in the path of the Hittite advances and begging for support from Egypt. Amongst the diplomatic correspondence remaining, are letters written on tablets some of which are addressed to Akhenaten and his 'daughter' Meritaten; and on the death of Amenophis III, to his widow Ty, who like Nefertiti, must have been aware of the growing unrest. That there are none remaining addressed to Nefertiti cannot be taken as evidence that she was not interested: so many were lost! Much learned work is still concentrated on those tablets we possess, to try and see Egyptian history through foreign eyes. But the language difficulties and foreign misunderstandings are innumerable.

It may well have been about this time that Akhenaten took the young woman Kiya from his harem, to be his 'beloved' wife (but not his 'Great Royal' wife). Nefertiti, even if saddened, would have recognised the need for the King to have a son. On the blocks of stone from the Amarna buildings found at Hermopolis, there are many scenes that we can but try to interpret in the light of our present knowledge. Names are obliterated (Kiya's) and some of the figures. Perhaps we shall gather more evidence from the British Museum excavations on this site (the modern Ashmunein). Later buildings are found on top layers, and some Amarna blocks would have been re-used. It is hoped that many more remain to be found from the earlier buildings, in the 'Amarna' layer of time. One thing is certain from the blocks we have, and that is that Kiya's name was erased from many of them, and/or overcarved by Meritaten's name and even Ankhesenpaaten's name. Maketaten is also named, so some must date to *before year twelve*, the last evidence we have of all six daughters being together, as apparently soon after this came the sad shadow of Maketaten's death. Tutankhaten's name (later Tutankhamen) also appears on the Hermopolis blocks: and repeatedly that of NefernefruatenNefertiti. This subject recurs in relation to the royal tomb.

There are several scenes of a trio on these Hermopolis blocks. The three people are unnamed but consist of a king, wearing a bulging war crown with an unusual heavily beaded edge of uraei that Akhenaten wore in the middle years of his reign, a lady wearing a rare type of wig pushed back off her brow, *without* the uraeus (or a crown) and a small child following her. They present a distinct family group. The art is of the cruder form of the earlier to middle years of the reign, and the trio could well be Akhenaten, Kiya and their child.

Two young daughters of the next generation are mentioned in these carvings, named after the two princesses Meritaten and Ankhesenpaaten (designated therefore 'the younger'). As mentioned before, these are linked with Akhenaten's name as though they are fathered by him with his daughters; but his daughters' names cover Kiya's name so it would seem likely that he fathered the children by Kiya. It could therefore be said that she also bore him his heir Tutankhamen. Besides Akhenaten's, the name NefernefruatenNefertiti appears repeatedly on the Hermopolis blocks. She is generally inscribed as the mother of her daughters in the usual way. But on one block, unfortunately broken, is her Aten name *Nefernefruaten* followed by *mry* 'beloved of' as on the Petrie Co-regency Stela described later, where it is followed by 'Akhenaten'. Although the bottom of the Hermopolis block is broken away we can make a pretty 'sure guess' that the name that followed the 'Beloved' here was also 'Akhenaten'. This related the cartouche to Akhenaten's co-ruler and later his successor - but we must not anticipate!

VII   The Famous 'Year 12'

In the twelfth year of the reign, two outstanding things happened inter-
rupting what seemed the calmness of Amarna days. One was an international
pageant at which the nations of the Empire gathered to bring tribute to Egypt
from their countries. The other was the visit of Queen Ty. Was her visit timed
near the international event to give extra point to both events? or was it the
clever, talented Queen Mother who stimulated the Aten-centred worshippers to
widen their contacts? As wife of Amenophis III, monarch of the Egyptian
Empire at its height, she must have had an understanding of the various mental-
ities of the neighbouring countries. It was not for nothing that their kings
wrote to her about international affairs at the death of her husband.

The tremendous international gathering must have been an emotional
affair. Akhenaten and NefernefruatenNefertiti were carried shoulder high in the
royal palanquin made of electrum, an alloy of silver and gold, gleaming in the
sun and graced by his personality and her beauty. Shade bearers held their rigid
semi-circular protective screens on long poles over the heads of the two monarchs, while the fan bearers nearer to them, waved their flowing feathers to
waft a current of air across them. (Fig. 23)

Once they arrived at the Hall of Tribute, they were seated on two thrones
on a platform under the canopy of a decorated pavilion. Their courtiers and
visiting ambassadors and envoys would approach them up a ramp. (Fig. 24)

Even at such a mixed and international gathering, we can see in the picture
that Nefertiti has her right arm around the King's waist and her left hand in his,
as they sit enthroned and watch the proceedings. Little more can be seen of her
on the far side of him than the streamers of her crown, her flowing sash, and
her feet beside the King's on the double hassock arranged for their comfort.
She is, of course, named in such scenes as NefernefruatenNefertiti and in the
interspersed hieroglyphic text, as the mother of their six daughters who stand
behind them.

The gathering must have been noisy and crowded, and the air heavy with
a mixture of smells, as streams of tribute bearers brought their gifts of incense

Fig. 23. Akhenaten and Nefertiti seated in the shining state palanquin

and other herbs, precious animals, hides and skins, furniture - a tremendous variety of gifts. (Fig. 25)

From the south lands of Africa, the envoys brought ingots of gold, and probably silver; elephants' tusks for the many ivory ornaments and the ivory inlays in ebony furniture which can be seen in the examples belonging to Tutankhamen. Their gifts of tame leopards, monkeys and enchanting gazelles were a sensitive tribute to the Egyptians' love of animals. Shields were included in the offerings, no doubt heavily decorated with native symbols and with accompanying bows and arrows, all brought from Nubia and the Sudan.

Also from the south, and the people of the 'north' (we should say the East) came musk and myrrh; sandlewood and spices, and scents for cosmetics, and incense to burn to the Aten. The bearded Syrians with their embroidered robes wrapped round their bodies, brought their valuable chariots and invaluable horses and weaponry. An antelope was included in their tribute, with an oryx, and a lion, perhaps tamed, as they were sometimes kept as a pharaoh's pet. Akhenaten, as mentioned before, did not hunt and kill like so many of his predecessors and followers. Metal bowls with lids decorated with models of animal heads were probably from the East, while double-handled amphora, decorated with lotuses and other flowers and buds on the rims, like those vases one can see in the Herakleion Museum in Crete, probably came from there.

Libyans, who wore side plaits from the crown of their heads and a feather stuck in their hair, brought ostrich eggs, and ostrich feathers for the Queen's

Fig. 24. The King and Queen with their six daughters at the pageant

73

Fig. 25. Foreign tribute bearers

fans and plumed head-dresses. The visitors are shown as very active and probably vociferous in their acclaim.

All these scenes are full of action, in row upon row of foreign visitors carved on the walls. They are carrying their gifts, pulling chariots, leading animals, carrying weaponry and the pelts and skins over poles on their shoulders, and also noticeably enjoying themselves. In one scene there is much roistering celebration, with people dancing, wrestling, being flung in the air while others clap their hands to the rhythmic beat of the tribal singing. A few, more orderly types, are raising their arms in jubilation. (Fig. 26)

The six princesses, in the only complete picture we have of them all together, are shown in two rows of three behind their parents. (Fig. 24) Meritaten is paying some attention to the ceremonies and, holding Maketaten by the hand appears to be trying, unsuccessfully, to get her to take an interest in them; but she has turned her back. She talks to Ankhesenpaaten who is holding something, perhaps a gift from the visitors. In the second row, the three youngest princesses are completely preoccupied with their own affairs. Nefernefruaten-the-Younger is patting what looks like a small pet she is holding, while Nefer-nefrure (the first to have Re included in her name instead of Aten) is holding a tiny gazelle, without doubt a gift to the children, which Stepenre, the youngest, appears to be trying to feed.

The second event was the visit of Akhenaten's mother, and inscriptions show she retained her title of 'Great Wife' of the King after her husband's death, which it would seem had probably occurred before this visit as she is not accompanied by him in any of the State visits and less formal celebrations extended to her by her son and daughter-in-law. Ty brought with her in her retinue her chief official Huya, Superintendent of her House, her Treasury and her Harem at her palaces at Malkata, Thebes, and also possibly in the Fayum oasis, which is south and slightly west of Cairo. Huya was accorded the honour of an investiture by the King and Queen who made him a 'person of gold', meaning, as noted before, the recipient of the award of 'Gold Collars'. His tomb in the cliffs, like all the rest of the noblemen's tombs there, was never

Fig. 26. Roisterers at Amarna

used. But it is our luck that a tomb was carved for him because, not surprisingly, Ty's man had many of the festivities of her visit inscribed on the walls, showing him as the factotum that he was, and it is from these that we get some of the fascinating, intimate details of her visit.

She was obviously welcomèd and celebrated with great personal honour and rejoicing. Her husband, Amenophis III, is only pictured in one small, solemn scene in a most insignificant position on a lintel over a doorway. He does not appear in the temple or banquet scene, for instance, where only Ty with 'King's daughter' Baketaten sit opposite Akhenaten and Nefertiti and their family. Amenophis III may have died, but in honour of being Akhenaten's parents, he and Ty are shown with Baketaten on this lintel. The Queen and princess sit opposite him, although in his lifetime the Queen would normally have sat beside him. She and Baketaten raise their right arms as though in a formal, funereal salutation, which he answers with a weary half gesture. Although Ty wears her high-plumed head-dress, he only wears a flat cap or wig-cover with a streamer and, of course, a uraeus on the brow. The Aten hands them both the Ankh (of eternal life?); as crowned heads, they are the only people apart from Akhenaten and Nefertiti to be given this direct award from the god.

Ty is normally pictured as loving wife to her husband and mother to her son, and not in kingly roles, although in Nubia she and her husband were cult figures. In Huya's tomb she bears the courtesy title of 'Hereditary Princess' (like Nefertiti, although apparently neither was of royal blood); and Ty is given the poetic chivalry of the phrase "Filling the place with Beauty" as she undoubtedly did: and the royal titles "Mistress of South and North, Wife of the King whom he loves; Lady of Two Lands", besides retaining her title of 'Great Royal Wife'. This last title was possibly retained by 'Great Queens' during their lifetime.

To balance the formal scene of Ty opposite her husband's portrait, Akhenaten and Nefertiti sit side by side on the other half of the lintel. He has an arm round her shoulders and Nefertiti, with one hand on his knee, turns fully round to look up into his face in a manner totally unlike any traditional royal scenes, in a flexible attitude even for the freedom introduced into Amarna art. She hails their daughters with her free hand, and it is almost possible to hear the chatter going on as the girls wave ostrich feathers and join in the conversation. It counter-balances but is in complete contrast to the sad scene with Ty. But the link is formed between *the two royal families*. Every honour was, paid to Ty. Akhenaten escorts her to the 'temple of the Aten in Akhetaten' (the inscriptions allow no mistake as to where it was!) and she was also provided with a 'sun-shade temple', a 'Shade of Re'. Outside the temple the grooms wait with horses at the ready, probably some from Ty's own stable because in the Petrie Museum there is a heavy limestone seal over six inches (15.2 cm.) long with a roughly formed but raised 'spine' on the back with which to grasp it; on the front, in the centre, is Ty's name in a cartouche, and this is flanked both sides by a spirited horse deeply carved in the stone. Each horse is surmounted by a lizard, the hieroglyph meaning 'many' - so Ty was rich in horses! Professor Smith has pointed out that this seal, so deeply and well cut, could have been used to impress the damp mud slapped on the bolts of the stables, when the grooms left for the night. The deep cutting would make a bold impression of raised shapes, leaving no doubt as to whose horses they were in the stable. The style of the stamped seals would resemble that of the mud sealings on the outermost door of Tutankhamen's tomb.

In the tomb of Huya, Queen Ty's factotum, there is a waterside scene which, although much damaged, immortalises the food gatherers. It shows birds being snared as they rise from the reeds in the marshes; cattle grazing by the river and a herdsman's hut or hide-out with a pile of food outside it. Fish are being caught in the river by a boatman, perhaps with a line, or net, or even one of the bottle-shaped fish traps with a wide opening at one end into which the fish swim on their way to the narrow, closed end! Besides the regular hunters and farmers, there are a number of tomb scenes in this dynasty which show family expeditions into the marshes. These were perhaps regarded as being rather exciting, being in a narrow papyrus boat surrounded by the high reeds and papyrus, with the father of the family fowling and fishing.

In one Theban tomb, there are two boats with such families aboard. The low, thin boats have a lotus bud and a flower at prow and stern, and are shown on the blue marsh which is full of fish and water-birds. In one boat the husband is spearing a leaping fish while his wife sits calmly on the flat little deck, but nevertheless clinging to his leg for support, while a servant stands at the prow holding a lotus in one hand and a caught bird in the other. In the second boat the father of the family is holding a brace of birds in one hand, and a throw-stick in the other, just before hurling it at a flight of birds rising out of the thicket. His wife stands admiringly behind him, and there are two young girls, possibly their daughters, with them. One holds lotuses and birds as she stands at the stern, and the other, oblivious of all the hunting going on above her, kneels and picks a lotus from the water.

In the British Museum there is a beautiful painting of this popular scene in which a striped cat, perhaps the trained family pet, is flushing the birds out of the thicket towards his master's raised throw-stick. Despite the inevitable hunting motif, a goose stands happily unassailed at the prow of this slender, unstable-looking, skiff-sized boat. Duck, teal, pigeons, and wild geese were netted or brought down with the boomerang-type throw-stick. Cattle are pictured at Amarna being hand-fed in mangers. Sheep, goats, pigs and oxen were all part of the diet. Well-carved joints of meat and poultry are shown on the Aten offering tables. No doubt venison was also enjoyed; there are many pictures of young deer in flight; desert animals of value included the antelope and oryx. Lettuces were cultivated and believed to have erotic powers, and of course all the delicious fruit available now - the sweet figs, and melons and huge luscious dates.

All this is not included in the scenes in Huya's tomb. Possibly the inclusion of food gathering at all in his tomb was to show that he was greatly honoured and was included with the palace staff during the visit of 'his' Queen Ty, and that as Ty's man, he shared the responsibilities. Some tact must have been necessary to include him and yet not disorganise or disgruntle the harmony of the regular officials at their valued tasks. It needed considerable training, overseeing, and wide administrative experience to organise the corps of food-gathers, cooks and palace servants, the food and drink required, and the musicians and decorative floral environment for such an event as the banquet for Ty, as described in the carved scenes.

As part of these celebrations, it is easy to imagine Akhenaten, processing through the palace with his quite extraordinarily beautiful wife and mother wearing their tall plumes and long gowns, at a reception for visiting ambassadors and statesmen. The royal party would have come over the bridge from their residence and down the ramp which led into the huge Broad Hall open to the sky. One of the unique architectural features of this palace was that the doorways between the State Halls were high up in the walls and approached by ramps; these were bordered on each side by carved stone balustrades of alabaster, sandstone, and black or red granite; this distinctive architectural feature was emphasised by the colour of the differing stones. The carved scenes on the sides of the balustrades, show the family worshipping the Aten with the inscriptions continuing over the broad curved top. The supporting walls formed the slope of the ramps, while the balustrades remained at a fixed height; nevertheless, *within* the carved scenes on the balustrades, the family are shown standing on either a gently rising or a falling line, *suggesting* their progress up and down the ramps.

Petrie found a large alabaster block of a balustrade in the place where the doorway had been between the Broad Hall of the palace and the first State Apartment. It is in the Petrie Museum, and on it, the line of the ground level is shown as a gently rising one, while on a Cairo block, the base-line on which the family stand is a descending line. This certainly indicates their undulating procession through the many palace halls of audience for some half a mile, probably to an ornately decorated throne-room at the end, with the golden rays of the Aten in a splendid inlaid scene. Coming from the Broad Hall, the family would ascend in stately procession to the high doorway (in the wall which once stood in the place where Petrie found the fallen balustrade) and then, pausing above the heads of the people, greet them, before descending into the next huge, columned State Hall where they would again 'appear' at the next doorway high above the heads of another audience. Was this echoing, with the rise and descent between each ramp leading to a doorway, the rhythm of the Aten in its rise and fall each day?

We have the incredible good fortune to be able to see in one of the tomb carvings, the royal family at a meal, in year 12 of their reign, some 3,300 years ago. So vividly are the records carved in the tomb of Huya that we can see what they saw, wore, ate and drank and enjoyed in each other's company. At a meal on the visit of Queen Ty, Akhenaten sits opposite her and his half-sister Baketaten, with his wife and children beside him. There is no centre table; each adult has a separate table of food and one of drinks by the side of their chair. (Fig. 27) The two Queens wear long, open pleated gowns and Queen Ty, a tall plumed head-dress over her wig, perhaps as a courtesy to her son and daughter-in-law in their palace, but they, perhaps out of respect for her, or for their own comfort, merely wear uncrowned wigs, but, of course, with the uraeus on them.

As a main course Akhenaten seems to be eating a kebab, with the meat strung round a large bone which he holds in his hand and bites, while Nefertiti is gazing at a small fowl which she raises in her hand. Whatever Ty was enjoying is missing, although she appears to be handing some morsel to Baketaten who sits beside her, but Ty may only have been gesturing conversationally with her right hand. In such meals, bread would have been available, and besides poultry and meat, the Nile fish, served no doubt on the elegant dishes

Fig. 27. The family dining with Queen Ty

of which fragments remain in the Petrie Museum. These are hollowed with shining-white glaze inside and a life-like painting of a fish glazed on the underneath side, with 'fins' protruding from the rim as handles. Some of the fragments of other dishes found by Petrie were of yellow gourds, perhaps for the lettuce, or cooked leeks, lentils or onions. These vegetables would have been ferried over fresh from the West Bank, and salt added to the vegetable oils in which they were cooked. The variety of fruits would have included pomegranates in season, and there were glazed dishes like melons, perhaps for serving the fruit. For the cakes, the flour would have been hand-ground on stone, with honey used as a sweetener - honey from the desert bees with their ferocious sting; they form part of the word for 'king'; and are part of the excavator's problems when they alight on him or her! Milk and water would have been available for the children, with jars of wine or beer for the adults. The wine was marked with the vintage in years of the reign, which is one of our sources for dating! More jars are ready on further side-tables to replenish the stocks. In the distance on the far side of the scene are two burners, perhaps with sweet-scented herbs or for keeping the food hot.

For the comfort of the diners, there were red hassocks for their sandalled feet, mounted on quite high decorated wooden footstools, so that their legs did not dangle to the floor. They varied in size for the convenience of each person: the King's being the largest, like his chair, and Queen Ty's slightly larger than Nefertiti's. Did the Queen Mother have bigger feet? Baketaten's hassock is very small, just right for her feet, but the two younger princesses only have slim cushions for their bare feet; perhaps they fell over the footstools for which their legs were far too short. Nefertiti's footstool overlaps Akhenaten's chair, so that although she is shown as sitting just behind him, enabling his activities to be seen, it can be taken that she sat beside him. The details in Nefertiti's home were carefully thought out and it was possible that her calm manner hid a competence which established an atmosphere that was peaceful as well as elegant. Perhaps this is what Akhenaten meant when he had inscriptions carved of her in which he describes her as "soothing the heart of the King in his house". (Fig. 27)

On a subsequent part of the wall scene, the party is shown in another room. The wall decorations are different although still inscribed with the names of those present. The scene probably takes place after dinner, as there are no food tables, and whereas at dinner Akhenaten only wore his pleated hip-wrap,

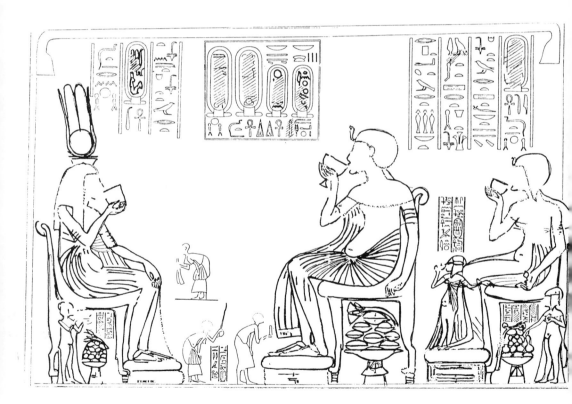

Fig. 28. After dinner refreshment

80

he has added a pleated robe and shoulder-wrap like the queens wear, possibly in the cool of the evening. The adults are drinking; Akhenaten from a stemmed goblet, while the two Queens tip handleless mugs to their lips, all probably of gold or silver, as have been found from other reigns, but alas none rescued from this one. Beside Nefertiti and Ty, there are baskets of fruit and cakes, which are much to the taste of the children. Baketaten is already eating something; the youngest, Ankhesenpa-aten, clings with one hand to Nefertiti's chair, and eats fruit(?) held in the other, whereas Meritaten, to show her age and independence is standing up beside her mother, with one fruit in her left hand while her right hand explores the piled up dish! By Akhenaten's chair the 'goodies' seem to be closed cakes or pastries. Everyone obviously had a choice. In front of Queen Ty, the pompous Huya raises his staff of office to the King: after all it was in his tomb! (Fig. 28)

Music was a constant accompaniment to banquets throughout the XVIIIth Dynasty. Amongst court musicians shown at Amarna, women predominate as players of the stringed instruments, although men are quite often pictured as playing large harps; and the familiar Egyptian scene of a blind man playing one as an accompaniment to a blind choir is also pictured. Eye disease is so frequent in the country one wonders whether those afflicted were taught music by ear to give them a position in the community; they are a singing, music-loving people.

One Amarna carving, now in a private collection in America, despite the block being completely broken away at the top, shows the average string quartet with a fifth woman present as chantress and leader, as she claps her hands to the rhythm. In this group, the front woman plays a seven-stringed, full-sized

Fig. 29. String quartet

harp apparently resting on the ground, and she is followed by two lute players, each with a plectrum to play the strings, probably of ivory, and attached to her lute by a cord. The fourth musician has a hand-lyre, with a charming end-piece carved like a cornflower: the fifth young woman is shown as the leader or singer.

Fig. 30. Foreign musicians

There was no shortage of musicians for the dinner party for Queen Ty. One carving of a quartet, which although broken, can be seen to be similar, if not the same group, as the one described above. (Fig. 29) The court musicians are proceeded by Huya, bowing and carrying his staff of office as he prepares to introduce them. One gets the feeling from his constant obeisances that perhaps Ty's Court was more formal (old-fashioned?), than at Amarna. There is also a group of foreign musicians, perhaps visitors to the pageant or members of Ty's household. (Fig. 30) These performers seem to be men wearing long, tiered skirts and a head-dress which tapers at the top and is tied round with a band. One man is plucking the strings of a very large lyre, almost as tall as he is, which is mounted on a broad base, the shape of a foreign, possibly Syrian, vase. It has an octave of strings. The desert-dwelling bedouin rather unexpectedly appear to have been the first to be pictured with such a lyre. Sometimes the frame is supported on models of gazelle's heads, but here another familiar desert design is employed - two rod-like spears. The picture of this gentle, civilised, musical environment is unique. Perhaps it was the cherished partnership of a King and his Queen Regnant that stimulated them to allow their private life to be demonstrated in such detail - so rare in what we have left from Egyptian scenes.

82

VIII   As Time Went On

It could be said that any change at Amarna was momentous; life there continued on its decorative course with the royal family as unquestioned leaders of the people, pursuing their religious, state and family life together, with the six princesses growing up to play their part. There were no rebellions; no revolutions. The courtiers' tombs continued to be carved with records of events for eternity, rather like, much later on, the early church mosaics illustrated the Bible.

But changes were beginning at Amarna, and some were of more significance than they appear. Nefertiti's name was prepared for mass reproduction, in two parallel cartouches, *like the two names which it is necessary for a king to have,* a move Queen Tawosret made in a later reign before she actually adopted two names as a king. Another change was made in the inscriptions, which may seem trivial, but it wasn't. In the writing of Nefertiti's ubiquitous title 'Great Royal Wife', the word normally used for 'great' was replaced by another of the same meaning. Both the Queen-monarchs, Hatshepsut and Tawosret, dropped *their* title of 'Great Wife' before they adopted their kingly titles, after the death of their respective husbands. But Nefertiti's name-changes began while Akhenaten was beside her and the normal word for 'great' was passed on to Meritaten as the eldest princess. It would seem that as time passed, Nefertiti assumed the two names of a king, so as to be *named officially* beside Akhenaten as co-regent. She took this step presumably knowing that it was similar to that of previous ruling queens.

But before this happened, the apparently serene course of this united family was arrested: sorrow struck at the heart of it with the death of the second daughter, Maketaten. The graphic scenes of the deep grief this caused are carved in her tomb, as described later, and it must have shaken the foundation of the family security, which had been built up by Nefertiti and Akhenaten. It was the first break in the routine which seems to have been as regular and steadfast as the rising of the sun in Egyptian mornings and its setting at night.

In one scene recording the change in Nefertiti's title in the later years, she stands before the seated Akhenaten and strains a liquid of some sort into an elegant, flat, metal bowl with a stem, which he holds out for it. (Fig. 31) It is not the usual shape of an Amarna drinking vessel and there were plenty of court officials to pour the King a drink if he wanted one; but this ceremony, performed by the 'Great Queens', is found in other reigns and appears to have

Fig. 31. Nefertiti as a 'Great Queen' offers a libation to Akhenaten

had a special significance, perhaps that of invoking long life for the king. If Akhenaten was ailing at this time, then the gradual changes being made in the names and titles of Nefertiti may well have been a natural progression in his plans to establish her officially as his co-regent. Curiously enough this same scene, perhaps semi-sacred, is also on an unfinished stela now in Berlin. The figures are merely outlined on it and not yet named, but as can be seen below, the standing figure looks like Nefertiti, and on to her *Khepresh* 'blue' crown the Aten is shining a ray, as the god does for her and Akhenaten. She pours liquid into a stemmed goblet, held out by a seated king just as Akhenaten does in the same kind of scene above, and from a similar situla-shaped jug. (Fig. 32)

In the next reign, their daughter Ankhesenamen (Ankh-es-en-Amen) stands in a similar pose in front of her seated husband, King Tutankhamen,

Fig. 32. Unfinished carving of ritual performed by 'Great Queens' for kings

who once again, as can be seen in Figure 33, holds out a stemmed vessel, but this one is so decorated with high ornamental flowers around the edge that no one could possibly drink from it! The young Queen is pouring from a similar little jug to that used by the other queens, the contents of which would barely cover the bottom of this large ornamental bowl, indicating that this was a ceremonial ritual. This is further borne out by it being on Tutankhamen's golden shrine.

Fig. 33. Tutankhamen's 'Great Queen' pours his libation

Then, Queen Tawosret, who succeeded her husband at the end of the XIXth Dynasty, is shown in just such a scene about to pour from a similar little jug into a stemmed goblet held out by her seated husband, Sethos II (Fig. 34) and this particular example of the ceremony may give us the clue to its meaning. The King holds in his other hand a fan-like object featuring the hieroglyph for 'million' and 'many', suggesting the object of the ceremony could have been connected with the King's long or eternal life. Queen Tawosret revered the affair so much she had it immortalised in silver. Clearly this was a ritual performed by Great Queens and the unnamed figure on the Berlin stela who looks like Nefertiti *was* Nefertiti, despite a once hazarded guess (without any evidence) that the unnamed figure was the 'youth' of whose *existence* there is still no proof.

Fig. 34. 'Great Queen' Tawosret pouring libation for King Sethos II

From later still, Petrie found on a broken little stone stela, now in his Museum, the ultimate proof of Akhenaten's co-regency with a woman; with someone 'Beloved' of him (one of Nefertiti's titles) and someone with Nefertiti's Aten name 'Nefernefruaten'. Here her name has a *new* name in front of it, to give her the ritual two names for a king. The new name is Ankhkheprure (Ankhkepru-Re), *which was at one time spelt as a feminine name*. On this co-regency stela, Akhenaten's two names, and those of Ankhkheprure and Nefernefruaten 'Beloved' of him are beside each other as a pair of kings, as co-regents are shown in other reigns. They appear in the same manner on a box from Tutankhamen's tomb with Meritaten also inscribed on it. Meritaten is described as 'Great Royal Wife' to her father; not an unusual title for the eldest of princesses to hold, and one which she inherited from Nefertiti who no longer used it *with the kingly titles*. After the death of Akhenaten the 'new' name, used with royal heraldry such as 'Son of Re', was understandably no longer spelt as a feminine name. It was retained with the throne name 'Smenkhkare' (Djeserkhepru), who could, alas, no longer be the 'Beloved' of her beloved Akhenaten, so she adopted another of her own titles, that of 'Beloved of the Living Aten'. So Akhenaten's *successor* was Ankhkheprure-Smenkhkare, 'Beloved of the Aten'.

All this time, preparations would have been going on for the royal tomb in the deep ravine of the cliffs; quarrying and carving all the walls was a huge job. Royal tomb furniture, Akhenaten's huge carved stone sarcophagus and those for Nefertiti and the princesses would all have been prepared, as well as the little 'Ushabti' figures, which were placed in the tombs to take the place of servants for the named owner in the 'next' world. The prayers for 'life eternal' were as constantly repeated in Amarna inscriptions as anywhere else, but the customs and decorations of the burial chambers were inevitably totally different from those of the ancestors of this royalty, and their followers. The sole worship of the Aten meant the omission of the many gods and goddesses that appeared on the walls of earlier and later tombs. They can still be seen at Abydos, for instance, in the wonderfully carved and coloured wall reliefs in the temple built by Sethos I in the next dynasty, the XIXth. Numerous gods and goddesses appear in these carvings, particularly Osiris whose shrine it was, with his wife Isis and their son Horus. At Amarna, as noted before, the myths and rituals of Osiris in the Underworld were abandoned and everything concerned with him, ignored.

Further back in time, in the Old Kingdom, the tombs of the courtiers were built around the pyramids of their king in their so-called 'mastaba' tombs. They were mostly robbed like the pyramids themselves. Having watched for days while one of the tombs was excavated, one realised just how thoroughly they were ransacked by the robbers. We watched as hundreds of alabaster vases were removed by the workmen from the top layers, whilst the sand was carried away in baskets on the heads of the girls. This was followed by the dig down the passage to the portcullis door which was finally raised and then - holding a candle to make sure there was some air in the interior, which had been closed for 4,000 to 5,000 years - we entered. Nothing could have been sadder than to have seen how the robbers had ravaged the place. They had known the way in, by cutting a hole in the stone at the bottom of the door, and nothing was left of the owner's hopes for the future: nothing of his burial equipment; only a few scattered remains of the occupant who was therefore denied even his name.

But fortunately on the walls of some of the most important of the Old Kingdom mastabas, carved scenes remain that are literally pictorial history books. There are beautiful carvings of the owner and his wife; his craftsmen making furniture and jewellery; herdsmen tending his flocks, driving his donkeys and chatting and arguing together - as the artists included many humorous asides in their inscriptions around the brilliant and beautiful pictures. One can see farmers scything the crops and winnowing the corn, and scribes recording the harvest. The owner is sometimes shown hunting in the marshes, with hippopotami and crocodiles in the water as well as fish. Rows of attendants bring tribute to him of loaves of bread, jars of 'good' wine and beer, and fresh vegetables, with plenty of aphrodisiac lettuces, and dancing girls for his amusement.

In the Middle Kingdom, about 2,000 B.C., the pyramid tombs of the kings were built further south than the pyramids at Giza and Saqqara. As time passed, power became more widespread in the community and the nobles were buried in their own localities, in tombs cut in the rocky cliffs of their own province, rather than as before, clustering around their king. But still their tombs were robbed and ravaged.

In the New Kingdom, before Amarna, big changes were introduced and the kings began to build their tombs on the West Bank of Thebes. Then Tuthmosis I started a new trend and hid his tomb in the valley *behind* the rugged cliffs, while building his mortuary temple in a different place, so as not to give away the position of the tomb. So many kings (and queens) followed suit that the valley is now known to the world as the Valley of the Kings (and Queens). The Valley of the Queens lies southwards from that of the Kings. But all in vain. Those who dug the tombs, and their children and grandchildren, knew where they were, and Tutankhamen's was the only one found relatively intact. Knowing how exquisitely lovely the rich ornaments, jewels and furniture from his tomb were, gives some idea of what the contents must have been like in those of the great pharaohs, for he was a young and relatively unimportant figure in the long history of Egyptian rulers.

Nothing was sacrosanct; the robbers took all: treasures of all sorts, boats, weapons, chariots, food, cosmetics, musical instruments, all were denied to the owners of the tombs, whose aim was to use them in eternity. In some cases efforts were made, perhaps by the priests, to save the tomb owners, and coffins were hurried to secret hiding places in the natural ravines in the cliffs, or reburied in someone else's 'House of Eternity', in the hope that they would not be entirely forgotten and their name would be spoken again. Egyptology has ensured that for them.

The hopes of the villagers for eternal life and the further use of their possessions were the same as those of the kings and statesmen; and thanks to the clean, dry heat of the sands of the Egyptian desert, their bodies, in their simple pit burials or in a pottery urn, were dried and preserved over the centuries. They took with them their sandals, sometimes domestic pottery, or perhaps a flint knife, some bread and a few glazed beads. In the Petrie Museum, there is a burial in an urn from *prehistoric* days, and therefore from uncountable thousands of years ago.

The difference in the carved illustrations in the Amarna tomb from those in other times, is a logical sequel to the supremacy of the Aten. But after Akhenaten's death, Tutankhamen began to restore Amen worship, which was continued by his military, non-royal successor, Horemheb. Gradually, Akhenaten became known as 'the heretic king' for his attempt to establish one creator from the many.

When the first viscious attack on Akhenaten's tomb took place, is not known; perhaps it was under Rameses II, who was a great builder and a great destroyer. For it was not only robbed, it was devastatingly destroyed in ancient times, surely under royal instructions. Since then the history of the tomb and its contents has been an unhappy one. Petrie wrote in 1892 that it had been 'found' by the local Arabs four or five years before, and rifled of all they thought saleable. They then sold the 'secret' of it to the Government. Officials visited it intermittently from Cairo in 1891/92, but in the meantime the local people, Petrie observed, were left to 'rake about without supervision'. Dr. Geoffrey Martin has set out these developments in the first volume of his book on *The Royal Tomb,* and his latest findings will be in the second volume. In his book, he has drawn every scrap salvaged from the floors of the tomb, the debris around it, and the stony floors of the valley, and illustrated the restorations from the pieces found, but he writes "the vengeance taken on it by the King's enemies was terrible" . . . "with few exceptions, none of the fragments was more than a few centimetres wide". Damage has continued in modern times. In 1930 A.D., it suffered from local feuds and up until 1972 destruction continued.

When Dr. Martin went to inspect the tomb in 1980, he expected total destruction; it was "almost," he wrote, "but not quite." He was amazed there was anything left on the walls to copy; but there was. He walked from the small town of Et Till, by the Nile at Amarna, across the plain to the cliffs (some 9 miles, 14 kms.) every morning for some weeks. He started before dawn, into the dark desert, but by the time he reached the entrance to the valley which leads by a side turning to the royal valley and the tomb itself, the sun was rising above the top line of the cliffs in which the tomb is cut, and the immense grandeur of the valley scenery was illuminated by it.

He describes Akhenaten's tomb as having steps leading down from the cliff-face with a smooth descending 'slide' in the centre for lowering the sarcophagus. A long sloping passage then descends to a similar second steep flight of steps leading to a kind of ante-room in which to rest the coffin, and possibly where prayers were spoken. This is confronted by a deep pit, in front of the actual burial chamber, which would have been dug *after a burial* as a protection against robbers; and possibly in a site like this, to act also as a well to drain off flood waters in the valley which would have poured down the sloping approach in a rainy season. In the burial chamber is the emplacement for the sarcophagus, which corresponds to the size of Akhenaten's as restored in Cairo. The Osiris mythology is replaced by carved wall scenes of the Aten and the life of the royal family, just as it is in the other cliff tombs belonging to the nobles at Amarna. But Martin writes that the scenes of the sorrowing family and mourners shown in the burial chambers have no equal; they are unique and unprecedented in their expression of the people's grief-stricken misery.

A very unusual feature in this tomb is a series of rooms which branch off the corridor before it reaches the pre-burial chamber pit. These rooms were evidently intended for the princesses, for the tomb of Maketaten, the second eldest daughter and the first of the family to die is there. The scenes of mourning carved on the walls of her tomb also have a real quality of grief, unsurpassed in any others found in such ancient reliefs, because the Amarna artists managed to convey an acute poignancy within a conventional framework. (Fig. 35)

Although there are two scenes with 'mourners' who adopt the formal gesture of raising their arms and clasping their heads, the artists have somehow shown a picture of real sorrow, unlike those groups of 'official mourners', in many burial scenes. Probably they were members of the Court and household who had known the girl and felt deeply about her death, and compassionate for her parents. Their sorrow is so imaginatively portrayed that it suggests the artists may have seen this funeral, and the grief expressed at her death. In two scenes, the royal couple stand together, with their right hands raised in despair to their crowns and Akhenaten half-turning to Nefertiti. In one scene, where they are bending over the child's figure on her bier, he clasps her wrist as though in

Fig. 35. Mourning for Maketaten

search of consolation for them both. In another scene he holds her arm.

In one picture, a woman is shown behind them carrying away a child sitting in her arms. It has been suggested that this might be Maketaten's baby fathered by Akhenaten and that she had died in childbirth. There is no evidence for this. Who was this child and what happened to it? It could in fact have been a younger brother or sister of Maketaten's born to Kiya. Another suggestion put forward, as incest was not taboo in royal circles, was that Meritaten as the official 'heiress', might have had a child by her father with the object of keeping the royal succession in the legitimate line, and that she, too, at her death, might have been buried in this tomb: no evidence remains however. The inscriptions and scenes on the Hermopolis blocks have already been described above. These children could have been Kiya's children by Akhenaten. Certainly Ankhesenpaaten was too young to have borne Tutankhamen. Was he not Kiya's son? And was this the reason, as has been suggested, why her name was denied her and overcarved by Meritaten's to 'register', as it were, an apparently 'legitimate' succession? The art in the royal tomb, although revised in some places, appears in the main to be that of the middle period of the reign, which accords with the 'trio' as described on the Hermopolis blocks - the figures of a crowned king with an uncrowned woman, and a child - who could well be Akhenaten, Kiya and their child.

In Dr. Martin's uniquely detailed study of every inch of the plundered and destroyed walls in the royal tomb, he discovered a number of hitherto unrecorded and unnoticed things, although other studies have been made of it. The King and Queen are occasionally shown, for instance, in an Aten temple; but in this instance, they are shown on one wall watching the sun rise and the animals and birds awakening to the dawn, while on the opposite wall is a scene of the Aten setting in its horizon, illustrating the Aten poem.

The inclusion in these scenes of obviously foreign visitors worshipping the Aten is typical of the singularly international outlook at Amarna. There is also another early instance of the idea of carving horses with their heads turned towards the onlooker, as in Figure 15. These full-faced animals remain on the damaged wall on which chariots were also carved, as they were on the walls of the noblemen's tombs.

But most amazing - or perhaps with what we know about Amarna it is not surprising - Dr. Martin found a second burial suite *on the same pattern as Akhenaten's own*. A tomb was cut for a second pharaoh in this one XVIIIth Dynasty tomb - presumably for the Pharaoh NefernefruatenNefertiti. The fact that this burial suite corresponded to Akhenaten's has been overlooked in the past because the approach corridor is curved. Dr. Martin perceived that this unusual shape was necessitated by the particular cliff formation, which was such, that had the corridor been tunnelled in a straight line it would have emerged again into the open valley. To avoid this the workmen swerved and burrowed inwards to the deeper part of the rock, causing the curve. This did not, however, prevent them from following the instructions given to them, to carve a burial suite of six rooms in the shape of Akhenaten's. Dr. Martin writes: "one thing seems certain: this suite of rooms, unfinished and completely undecorated represents a royal tomb within a royal tomb". He suggests that this second big tomb was begun for Nefertiti perhaps late in the reign when she was accorded "additional status as Regent" (to Tutankhamen) "or even sovereign". (*Illustrated London News*, September 1981) Down the similar steep entrance-steps of the second tomb came the sloping corridors which brought one to the burial chamber in which, although it was still undecorated, there was an emplacement for the sarcophagus. Was Nefertiti actually buried here? Dr. Martin thinks possibly yes. The walls were unfinished, but part of the floor was levelled. The protective pit, however, was not dug as is usual *after* a burial.

Amongst objects said to have come from the tomb is a gold ring inscribed with Nefertiti's long name, and the feet of a *ushabti* figure which described her as 'Great Royal Wife', with her name NefernefruatenNefertiti within the cartouche. But so many and so varied, and some so obviously fabricated are the stories of what was found outside the tomb, and so complete were the robberies, that it is difficult to be sure of the origins of the objects - or the tales. Certainly a *ushabti* figure named for her, not being prepared in a stone-carver's workshop but found near the grave, points to her burial there.

Certainly Maketaten must have been buried in this tomb. Fragments of a sarcophagus show at its corners her mother's figure instead of the four particular goddesses always found in this position, in other regions.

Was Nefertiti's body hurried to a safer resting place by loyal priests or courtiers; or had they passed on to 'eternal' life when the first assault was made on this royal tomb? It would not have happened in the time of Tutankhamen or the Amarna nobleman Ay, although the worship of Amen was by then restored. Horemheb usurped some of his predecessor Tutankhamen's statues, in a manner quite customary for a ruling pharaoh. He was the last king of this dynasty. After him came the Ramesside kings and many blocks of the actual Amarna buildings were re-used by Rameses II at Hermopolis. We should learn more in time from the British Museum excavations there. Whoever was responsible for the desecration of the tombs and the demolition of the furniture, their aim to destroy the identity of the owners and prevent their names from being spoken in eternity was a complete failure, and as dismal as their actions. We do not know who *they* were. But the world will not forget Akhenaten or Nefertiti.

We do not know either where Akhenaten's body found a resting place; or if it did. Neither do we know where Nefertiti is buried. There is a tomb in Thebes numbered 55 which was superficially excavated early in this century, when it had already been damaged by flood waters through a crack in the ceiling. It had been used as a *cache* for other royal burials, presumably desecrated and scattered. Some 'magic bricks' of Akhenaten's were found; a shrine belonging to Queen Ty, his mother; some canopic jars, all clearly from a royal burial. But of the actual burial there, damaged by water, with the inscriptions altered in ancient days, and the gold coffin probably designed for one person and used for another - we have little to help us identify it. Controversy over it has raged through the years and still continues. Gradually the bodies of some of the people whom Egyptologists at different times have believed were the occupants, have been located elsewhere. Tutankhamen was one; Queen Ty another: was it Akhenaten, Kiya, one of the princesses, or even Nefertiti? The only factual evidence registered by the excavators was that the body was laid out like a woman, with one arm across the chest and the other by the side, instead of both being folded across the chest like a king. Work on the enigmatic fragments of inscribed, gold strips from the coffin is continuing.

IX   The Spell of Amarna

Akhenaten's death must have been a searing experience in the rather enclosed Aten community, as is shown by the evidence of unprecedented scenes of grief in the carvings on the walls of his tomb. Nefertiti, after one of the closest and most loving royal partnerships to be recorded in history, had now to face her personal sorrow and her responsibilities as successor. On his sarcophagus, which was smashed up in the tomb, and therefore some time after his burial, she remains pictured as the supreme royal figure; unchanged from the original carvings, and unreplaced by any of the names of people who have been suggested as Akhenaten's successors, she is shown as the sole ruler. In this case, the continuance of the royal line rested on her care of Tutankhamen and his upbringing from the age of five or six, until his eventual marriage to one of her daughters, while steering a course of peace in the country.

The policy of the gradual establishment of her official regality with Akhenaten, which must have been agreed between them, was a strong one, and apparently successful. Despite the potential causes for rebellion at the death of Akhenaten, because he made Atenism the State religion in place of Amen worship, we find no evidence of chaos or confusion. Nefertiti's partnership with him must have helped her to pursue the pharaonic role alone. She would have been supported by a corps of loyal Amarna statesmen, and have had recourse to the advice and help of Ay, the senior statesman and possibly a relative.

There is a very revealing pair of gold ornaments from Tutankhamen's tomb which apparently date from the early months of her succession. On one of these is engraved the name of the co-regent Nefernefruaten with the *name of the Aten partly reversed in a way it was never written except in Nefertiti's name:* and, it is reversed to face a *kingly* image at the bottom of the cartouche. This pharaonic figure wears the regalia of the king's beard strapped on, and it is accompanied by a king's sceptre. On the other ornament of the pair is the new personal name Ankhkheprure, which was adopted by Nefernefruaten (Nefertiti), and the new title 'Beloved of the Aten'. The use of this new *title* instead of the usual one 'Beloved of Akhenaten', together with the name Nefernefruaten, suggests that this was engraved after his death, but before the actual coronation had taken place, and the throne name of Smenkhkare had been adopted for use with the new title. Royal burials took months to complete - seventy days for the embalming alone - but new insignia would be in preparation for the successor.

There is no record of the coronation except on the bricks of the so-called Coronation Hall of the Central Palace. This was of a rare design at the southern end of the palace and not in line with the central building. Pendlebury describes it as having been built over the debris of rubbish pits, and pits for trees, with the subsequent and necessary 'levelling' very badly done. He wrote that the whole affair was clearly "a 'rush job' for a special occasion". On the bricks of this rushed job, perhaps built during the months awaiting Akhenaten's burial and immediately after it, the only name found is Ankhkheprure (written at one time as a feminine name).

Nefertiti apparently chose to live in the palace which it would seem was the one Akhenaten vowed he would build for her, at the northernmost tip of the plain, surrounded by a wall some three feet thick.

The throne name Smenkhkare has been found on the carvings from the ceremonial gateway, with fragments in which the names of Akhenaten and Meritaten also occurred. But in the 1930s this greatly puzzled John Pendlebury, because the name 'Smenkhkare' was *still* attached to the unknown 'youth', so he questioned why Nefertiti's name was missing from her own gateway! Why indeed, unless it was she as 'Smenkhkare' who was there all the time! Pendlebury records that the many clay wine-jar sealings found were mostly sealed with Nefertiti's name, and the rest were nearly all inscribed with 'The House of the Aten'.

The early excavators recognised that this great building behind the huge wall 'gave monumental significance' to the north entrance of the city. It was destroyed in ancient times like the main buildings in the central city. But these ruins also lay in the pathway of the torrents of water that in rainy seasons rush down from the hills and swing round behind it, to the edge of the Nile. It had been plundered for stone, and for the mud-bricks which decay into a useful manure; and it is now partly covered by cultivated land. Alas, it has only ever been summarily excavated, and yet here must surely lie information about the latest years of the reign.

Fragments of carvings of some of the door jambs show Nefernefruaten-Nefertiti's name replacing Akhenaten's.

Painted plaster fragments, which had fallen from a 'window-room' above the central gateway, were reconstructed as far as possible by Ralph Lavers. They show a crowned, willowy and feminine-looking figure driving a chariot, *followed* by a considerably smaller crowned figure driving a chariot, with smaller horses. Both figures are under the Aten's rays; both figures wear a king's blue war-crown; but the second figure is smaller in comparison with the first, than Nefertiti is usually shown when she drives out *beside* Akhenaten in scenes in the central city. The impression given is that it could be the princeling Tutankhaten, when very young, following Smenkhkare - that is - Nefertiti.

Eventually Tutankhaten returned to Thebes. At Amarna the buildings were boarded up and the noblemen's tombs remained empty as the Court moved with the King. Tutankhamen's coronation ceremony was held in Thebes, in the temple of Karnak. He set about restoring Amen worship and this god's monuments (that Akhenaten had destroyed), and changed his name to Tutankh*amen*, while his wife, the third Amarna princess, Ankhesenpa-*aten*, who became his queen, changed hers to Ankhesen-*amen*. Then the young King died, possibly before he was quite twenty, and he left no heirs. The young Queen remained on the throne alone. In Tutankhamen's tomb, the 'God's Father' Ay is shown enacting the burial rites for him as a successor would do. He and Ankhesenamen are shown on a piece of gold foil saluting the King as he swings the scimitar over his head in the traditional scene of the conquering king, while grasping the hair of a foe kneeling before him, awaiting the fatal blow - the scene peculiar to pharaohs in which Nefertiti was pictured early in the reign. Their names are also together on a ring and although he was old enough to be her grandfather, he may have 'married' her to share with her the protection of the royal line. Then the old nobleman died, and the Queen was faced with the dilemma of maintaining the legitimate line of succession which she must have been brought up to revere.

The text of a letter is known to us from this time which was addressed to the King of the Hittites, Suppiluliumas. It is from a young widow, whom it is now thought can only have been Ankhesenamen, asking the Hittite King to send one of his sons to marry her, saying that she would then make him pharaoh. Suppiluliumas was sceptical, and small wonder. It was against Egyptian tradition to suggest a foreign prince should be their pharaoh. But the Queen, on the other hand, would know that Horemheb, who had been her husband's General-in-Chief of the Army and probably also his advisor, must have seen that his chances of succeeding to the Egyptian throne were becoming brighter.

After considerable parleying between the Queen and the Hittite King, he did at last send his son. He was murdered en route!

We now know that Horemheb became the next King, the last of the XVIIIth Dynasty. As noted before, Dr. Martin's excavation of Horemheb's fine tomb at Saqqara indicates that he strengthened his position on the throne by marrying a sister of Nefertiti, although she was appreciably older than he was. At one time it was thought to be Nefertiti who wrote to the Hittite King after

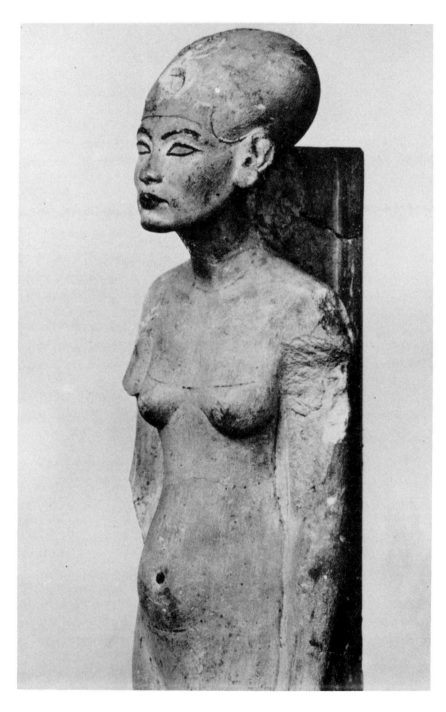

Plate VI. Nefertiti as an ageing monarch; for once
alone and without her family

the death of Akhenaten, for one of his sons to be made pharaoh; but she was a pharaoh; probably past child-bearing, and only anxious to establish Tutankhamen and her daughter.

But in these years when Amarna was no longer the capital of Egypt, we have no actual records of Nefertiti: where she stayed - possibly it was there; or how much longer she lived; or indeed what happened to her burial. But somewhere, sometime we shall find more evidence of these years. They are at the end of an historical era; but not at the end of the search for its history about which there is so much more to discover, and in which such a vital interest is shown. In the meantime, not surprisingly for Nefertiti, we are left with something we have again to describe as unique, as is so often the case at Amarna. Perhaps this is one of the particular charms of the period which, despite our doubts and disagreements about some of the less well-known happenings, draws all of us who have studied it back to it like a magnet.

This particular focus of our attention is a statue of Nefertiti, ageing and alone. (Pl. VI) Her hands, carved in detail, are hanging by her sides. No longer is one held by Akhenaten, nor is one held out to a small child-princess, both typical gestures of hers in Amarna statues and statuettes. Her shoulders stoop, her breasts' now sag a little: and the tell-tale lines of age are carved from the nostrils down the cheek, and from the corners of the mouth to a small bony chin.

Just as the famous art treasure in West Berlin of the head of NefernefruatenNefertiti wearing her particular crown is a gift to us of the portrait of the young Queen, so the finely carved little statue in East Berlin of the figure of NefernefruatenNefertiti wearing a *pharaoh's* crown, is a gift to us of her alone, as an ageing monarch, surely King Ankhkheprure-Nefernefruaten alias Ankhkheprure-Smenkhkare.

PART II

CLEOPATRA THE GREAT
King of Egypt

Plate VII. Cleopatra as 'Isis'; temple of Denderah

I   Cleopatra – 'Queen of Kings'

Right at the end of the list of eminent women in ancient Egypt comes one who needs only to be named to be known - Cleopatra. She had the titles of a pharaoh, but not the blood of an Egyptian, being a Greek from Macedonia, a region in the north of Greece. Despite the wonderful poetry and prose which has surrounded her name, the actual history, although not always the same as the romances which have been woven, proclaims her outstanding greatness as a person.

It was by chance that the name of Cleopatra (an earlier queen and ancestor) helped in breaking the code which led to the understanding of hieroglyphs and eventually to the reading of them as a language. But it was not by chance that Cleopatra the Seventh - known to all of us as just 'Cleopatra', was King of Egypt. "Descended of so many royal kings",[1] as Shakespeare wrote in *Antony and Cleopatra*, she was the last of the Greek ruling Ptolemies. She was the beloved mistress of the two greatest men of the day - both Romans - Julius Caesar and later the younger Mark Antony.

There is evidence that the fascination by which she held people would not have been from beauty alone: indeed she was apparently not a great beauty. But her grace of body and charm, great intelligence and companionship were to outlast passion. Shakespeare was to write "age cannot wither her nor custom stale".[2] The fate of the Mediterranean world of their day circled round the heads of these three people - two Romans, and the King of Egypt, Cleopatra, later named by Antony 'The Queen of Kings', as overruler of other eastern monarchs and their lands.

It is thought that the genes we inherit may have more to do with the make-up of our personalities than our environment. Unlike Nefertiti, about whose early life we know so little, we have some knowledge of Cleopatra's forebears - not at all a promising start! In and around them we can see the world of their day. Without the modern horrors of hijacking, machine-guns or bombs, there were the territorial ambitions, political and family intrigues, and many murders. Although the Ptolemies were Egypt's Greek rulers, the country was still in name, a sovereign state of great wealth, but the Ptolemaic rule had weakened, and by the time of Cleopatra's reign it was becoming more and more dependent on imperial Rome. Sulla, the Roman dictator in 80 B.C., was powerful and exerted a subtle overlordship of Egypt. He engineered the accession of Ptolemy XI to the throne of Egypt, though he was only a nephew of the previous King. Then Sulla decreed that Ptolemy should marry his step-mother who had been ruling in an interim period. Nineteen days after that, Ptolemy had her murdered! Then the people of Alexandria, claiming a right in the selection of their king, murdered him. This was how Cleopatra's father, Auletes, reached the throne, as Ptolemy XII.

In the aftermath, there was fear in Alexandria of Sulla's possible anger over the murder of Ptolemy XI, because it might have tempted Rome to annex the kingless country. Thus it was, that Auletes, the youthful son of a concubine in Syria, was urgently sent for to be king in 80 B.C. He was to become Cleopatra's father. It was possible for sons of concubines to reach the throne of Egypt and when Auletes, the illegitimate son of Ptolemy IX married his royal sister, he strengthened his position on the throne. At the same time, he quickly stressed his link with his father by adding the title 'Philopater' (lover of his father) to his name.

Near the end of year 70 B.C., Cleopatra was born. That sentence is misleadingly simple when one considers the dramas involved. Auletes appears to have had six royal children whose lives are interwoven with history. The two eldest, Cleopatra VI and Berenice IV were the daughters of Auletes' sister and first wife, Cleopatra V, who was possibly, if not certainly, also the mother of Cleopatra VII, known just as Cleopatra. How many people today know she was the Seventh of that name? Cleopatra is enough to call her to mind. Meanwhile, her mother disappeared from the scene, to be succeeded by a second wife of Auletes, who bore him another daughter, Arsinoe IV, and two sons, Ptolemy XIII and XIV. The boys were later to be successively associated with Cleopatra on the throne, but not for long: neither survived adolescence. (Fig. 36)

Cleopatra probably had a clear, olive complexion, rather than the fair, blond image created by some modern artists. Not only did she have the blood of Greek-Macedonia in her veins, where there was a mixture of peoples from earlier centuries, but possibly also Iranian and even Syrian blood from ancestral, Ptolemaic marriages with ruling royalty in the Near East. But her full regality stemmed from the Greek conqueror, Alexander the Great, who rescued Egypt from the domination of the Persians, and who was followed on the throne of Egypt by all the twelve Greek kings named Ptolemy. There were many inter-family marriages amongst the Ptolemies, tending to double family genes, both dull and brilliant. Cleopatra was not dull. She was fully capable of

CLEOPATRA's IMMEDIATE FAMILY

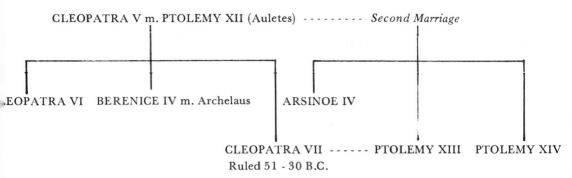

CLEOPATRA V m. PTOLEMY XII (Auletes) - - - - - - - - - *Second Marriage*

..EOPATRA VI   BERENICE IV m. Archelaus   ARSINOE IV

CLEOPATRA VII - - - - - - PTOLEMY XIII   PTOLEMY XIV
Ruled 51 - 30 B.C.

Fig. 36. Family tree

understanding the significance of the changing world in which she matured; the age of the expanding Roman Empire. This had already spread over Asia Minor (Turkey) and into the Near East, and Egypt must have appeared to the Romans as a ripe plum for their next expansion. This daughter of Auletes appears to have inherited her father's determination and, from the crudely cut portraits of her on metal coins, we can see a similarity in their strongly featured noses which both turn down at the tip. (Pl. VIII). It also seems that they shared an ambition to rebuild the Greek Empire as it had been under their ancestor, the world conqueror, Alexander the Great.

Cleopatra was the only one of the Ptolemies who mastered the language of the land she ruled, and she did not stop at that. Plutarch, the Greek historian, who was born only 76 years after her death, and who had access to information through his grandfather, wrote that she spoke several African and also eastern languages, including Hebrew and Aramaic - eight in all, he relates, besides her own native Greek. The fact that Auletes had her taught these foreign tongues, and that she was willing and able to master them, shows that they were both looking further abroad than the shores of Egypt.

Plate VIII. Cleopatra on a coin

In about 60 B.C., while Cleopatra was still a girl of ten years old, Auletes went to Rome to seek financial help to keep him on the throne. At this time, three men: Pompey, Julius Caesar and Crassus, were virtually ruling the Roman world - and Caesar was the most intelligent of the three. They agreed to support Auletes, but at what a cost. Impossible as it is to assess today, it certainly ran into many millions of pounds, as we know them, which of course put the Egyptians further into the hands of Rome. While Auletes was away his two daughters, Cleopatra VI and Berenice IV (apparently Cleopatra's full sisters), were alternately hailed as monarchs by differing factions in Egypt. The young Cleopatra must have viewed her sisters' disloyalty and the disorder in her father's affairs with dismay. Having learnt Egyptian, she must have known that the leading Egyptians disliked the Greeks, while as a Greek, she must have been aware that in the great cultural centre of Alexandria, the Greeks viewed the growing grip of Rome with fear and hatred. None the less she remained loyal to her father throughout his life.

Berenice seems to have gained in the leadership stakes during her father's absence, but as Ptolemaic queens did not rule without a male co-regent, a bride-groom was chosen for her. She had him strangled within three days. She then married Prince Archelaus from Asia Minor. But as he was a 'Pretender King' of Egypt, Pompey's forces marched against him under Gabinius in 55 B.C., and Archelaus was killed in a battle, in which the brilliant cavalry charge was led by a young Roman officer. Auletes ordered Berenice to be executed. What Cleopatra, now in her teens, thought of the execution of one sister and the disloyalty of the other, leaving her the heir-apparent to the Egyptian throne, can be imagined.

The young cavalry officer of the small but victorious Roman army that defeated Prince Archelaus gave the fallen Prince an honourable burial because he had formerly enjoyed his hospitality. This pleased the Alexandrians, as did the officer's protection of disloyal Egyptian prisoners from Auletes' vengeance. The officer's name was Mark Antony. Cleopatra probably first met him at this time when she was 15 and he nearing 30. Auletes regained full control of his throne, but in 52 B.C., although he was only 50 years old, he died, probably weakened by a burdensome and somewhat licentious life. An inscription remains in which he "hopefully" (hopelessly could he have but known) proclaims his children as lovers of each other (Philadelphoi). In his Will, Cleopatra, now 18, was proclaimed successor with the elder of her two half-brothers, Ptolemy XIII, who was then only 10 years old. Her first year as a Pharaoh was 51 B.C.

It is difficult to see this woman other than as a ruler, who from then on became inevitably entangled in world politics, particularly in Rome and the Near East. Trying to find a balance between the histories written about her over the ages, and the fiction which is equally variable, becomes a tight-rope journey. Some artists have idealised her beauty, which was possibly one of her lesser attractions; others have portrayed her as kittenish and coy, which does not fit in with the strength of her diamond-cut-diamond nature. It was the gleam of her personality which attracted people, and her wits that defeated Antony again and again in their youthful escapades. Some historians have seen her struggle as a bid to return Egypt to its former power and achieve a Greek-ruled Egypt in partnership with Rome, and have attributed this to power-seeking greed and selfishness. Others see it as a token of her Greek and Egyptian loyalty, later leading to a fight for the security of her children. Some-where between these major interests lies, unspoken, the thinking, inner nature of this woman: brave, a great lover and, typical of her times, one who did not prevent the death of her enemies or indeed mourn them.

She took a great pride in her appearance and her use of cosmetic aids became a part of the presentation of her graceful self. She actually studied the knowledge of the fragrant and protective mixtures which had been built up since Queen Hetepheres in the pyramid days nearly 3,000 years earlier. She used the oils and balsams for the protection of her skin against the hot, dry, desert winds and Egyptian sun, and delighted in the exotic perfumes. Her royal pride in the riches of her environment, looked upon by the Greeks and Romans as the voluptuous, oriental splendour of a designing woman, was a continuation of the magnificence that preceded her. They did not know of the Temple of Amenophis III at Thebes, embellished centuries before, of gold throughout and floored in silver; or the beauty of the inlays of Amarna; of the silver, gold, ala-baster and lapis lazuli, which had been used for thousands of years, not only for the royal jewellery, but also for vases and household objects of great beauty. Shakespeare was to write of our own Henry IV "uneasy lies the head that wears the crown". Cleopatra suffered from much envy, at the same time as being immensely admired. She was politically suspected and hated, but personally respected and honoured - and loved beyond belief. Hers was a personality about which no feelings were mediocre. She was considered enchanting and held in awe by the world despite the varying evaluations.

Like Hatshepsut and Nefertiti, Cleopatra was entitled 'Lady of the Two Lands' although also recorded as 'King'. Beginning her reign in the declining years of Ptolemaic power and well aware of Egypt's heavy debt to Rome, she was quick to introduce various astute financial measures. She proceeded - as some of her predecessors had done - to devalue the actual metal content of Egypt's silver and bronze coins by having lesser metals added to them. But she thought of something her predecessors had missed. She had the *numerical value* of the coins stamped on them, as we do, to avoid them being devalued by dealers because of their actual metal composition.

The Egyptians had been inclined to complain they were worse off than the Greeks in their own country, but the balance had been redressed to some extent by the kings who immediately preceded Cleopatra. For instance, the Rosetta Stone, now in the British Museum, immortalises the coronation of Cleopatra's great, great-grandfather, Ptolemy V, which, as a salute to Egypt he celebrated in Memphis, rather than the Greek city of Alexandria. There is a long decree carved on it promising such benefits as relief of taxes, amnesty, the restoration of temples and the setting up of a regular army and navy. As kings, the Ptolemies had long associated themselves with the god Amen-Re; and they accepted Egyptian symbols of royalty, such as the crook and flail carried by kings. They also wore the Pharaonic crowns with the cobra as an emblem of royal power.

Cleopatra wore the vulture head-dress of a royal 'Heiress' and she very closely and increasingly associated herself with the goddess Isis. (Pl. VII) This particular connection with the past was continued by the Ptolemies adopting the old custom of brother-and-sister 'marriages', just as the goddess Isis married her brother and husband, the god Osiris. Cleopatra stressed the wife, and later the mother appeal of this goddess, and mother of Horus. The Egyptians could identify her with their past religion and royalty, and as mentioned before, she 'spoke their language'. She diplomatically associated herself with her father's restoration of a number of temples, including the temple at Denderah of Hathor, who was identified as the goddess of love, with whom she appears. Travellers today can see this impressive temple, with much Greek architectural restoration of the Egyptian myths - and can see it almost whole.

But Cleopatra went even further in religious identification than her forebears by actually attending the highly esteemed religious rights of the Apis Bull, whose festival was held in Memphis in 51 B.C. In these holy-of-holy ceremonies, she alone is hailed as 'King'; the young boy, Ptolemy XIII, co-opted on the throne is not mentioned. She led, in person, on the sacred vessel itself, the important river ceremonial procession to Hermonthis, near Thebes. This must have endeared her to the loyal royalists of Upper Egypt, seeing her appear as part of their sacred, religious ceremonies. And it is notable that it is her head alone which is impressed on the coins of this period, without that of her co-regent, half-brother, Ptolemy XIII.

Egypt was a rich country, the biggest grain producer in the Mediterranean world; rich in vegetable oils; exporter of papyrus, the paper of the day; and also of linen. It is sad that with Cleopatra's skills, she inherited her kingdom at a time when it had become so increasingly dependent on Roman politics and conquests, to which she had always to give her unrelaxed attention. She was well aware of jealousies in her own country, so instead of being free to devote her active mind to improving social conditions in Egypt, she had constantly to turn her mind to the shifting sands of politics.

She seems to have been well aware of the danger of a Regency Council being set up to support the minor figure of her brother against her. She was right. Numerous of her female Ptolemaic ancestors had been powerful figures as consorts and one, briefly, even as a monarch. It is possible that at the age of 19 or 20, the dangers of her position may have stimulated Cleopatra to advance too quickly towards the image of herself as sole ruler. This was feared by the Romans who were always wary of an uprising against them in their dominions, and by the Alexandrians who feared that she might follow her father's subjugation to Rome: they seem to have been utterly unrealistic about the debts Egypt already owed. However, Cleopatra's rule was at this time actively interrupted by events abroad, as well as at home. Rome had been completely defeated by the Parthians in their empire, east of Syria, and Crassus, the third member of the ruling Roman triumvirate, with Caesar and Pompey, had been killed there. This threatened Rome's recently acquired kingdom of Syria and the new Roman governor there, Marcus Bibulus, hurriedly sent his two sons as envoys to petition Cleopatra for some of the Roman soldiers in Egypt. But the Roman troops who had settled in the country preferred to remain there and they murdered the young envoys. Cleopatra had the murderers put in chains, and had the bodies of Bibulus's sons sent back to their father to show her sympathy. This was unpopular with the Roman army who were responsible for the murder and with the Alexandrians who looked upon her action as a pro-Roman move. In fact Cleopatra's compassionate attempt to console Bibulus for the loss of his two sons, greatly endangered her position, if not her life.

Egypt had just suffered an extremely bad harvest from a spectacularly low Nile, and in 50 B.C. a crippling decree was issued, most unusually including the name of King Ptolemy as well as Cleopatra, and obviously stemming from Ptolemy's supporters. It ordered that all grain should go to Alexandria, and none to Middle or Upper Egypt (areas loyal to Cleopatra). It was possibly issued to avert the danger of famine in Alexandria, which would have been bad enough for her, but the main significance was that it had been the work of Ptolemy's Regency Council, who were taking the reins of government into their own hands. Caesar wrote in his book *The Civil War*, that the Queen was forced to leave Alexandria, and she fled to Upper Egypt, the very area that had been denied their share of the crop. But she 'spoke their language' and they remained loyal to her. In Rome conditions were worsening. During the Civil War, Caesar had conquered Pompey who was exiled, and he eventually journeyed to Egypt. According to Caesar's account, by this time the Council and favourites of the young King Ptolemy XIII had virtually taken command of Egypt, and they now became afraid that Pompey might try to seize the country. They sent Achillas, an officer of the King, to welcome Pompey, who was courteously received but as he disembarked from a small boat, Achillas had him promptly murdered. It is understandable why, after seeking 'refuge' in Upper Egypt, Cleopatra decided to follow the precedent set by her exiled ancestor, Cleopatra IV, and go abroad. She went to Ascalon (Ashkelon), a Ptolemaic Philistine city on the coast north of Gaza, nearly opposite where Ptolemy had his forces ready for action at Pelusium, the easternmost fortress gate of Egypt, near the modern town of Damietta. (Fig. 37) Cleopatra gathered local help from the region, where like her father her image was on the coins. But then a great moment in world history occurred. Caesar landed in Egypt - only four days after the death of Pompey in 48 B.C. It was the turn of the tide for Cleopatra.

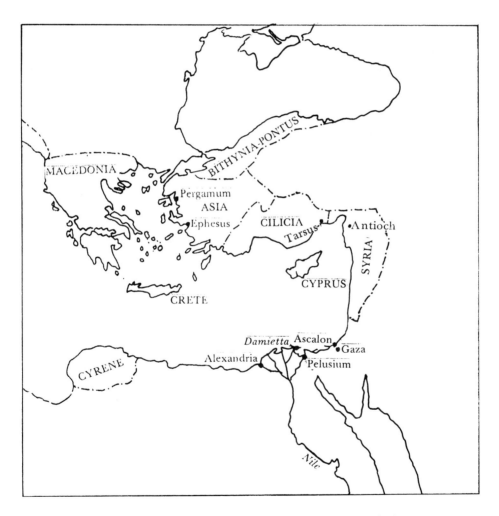

Fig. 37. Map of Eastern Mediterranean in Cleopatra's day

II   Cleopatra and Julius Caesar

Once again a Roman ruler was met by a leader of Ptolemy's Court; indeed Caesar was offered Pompey's severed head. Perhaps Ptolemy's tutor, a eunuch called Pothinus, hoped that Caesar would take fright and go away. If so, it shows the paucity of the Council's thinking. Caesar did not take fright; and he had no intention of going away. Egypt was rich and owed him money that he needed for his wars. He was also greatly concerned, as a former supporter of Auletes, to cement the decree in his Will, by resettling Cleopatra on the throne again *with* Ptolemy XIII. This was a condition that Auletes had laid down and had called upon the Romans to support, and of which Caesar doubtless thought Pothinus needed reminding.

He sent abroad for Cleopatra, who had lost no time in getting a letter to him, and her return was soon accomplished. Plutarch reports that she set sail at night in a little boat, with only one of all her friends, and landed hard by the palace at Alexandria. A fleet would have been blocked by Ptolemy at sea, but in this way she somehow slid through into the harbour. How she managed to land is the basis of a number of stories, in the way that a number of stories arose out of so much of her momentous life. One such story claims that she bribed Ptolemy's guards, which would not have been too difficult. But Plutarch writes that she was smuggled ashore in a carpet tied round with a leather thong, which her one friend, Apollodorus, carried on his back to Caesar in the palace. Caesar must have been appalled by the indignity of her plight and fascinated by her bravery and spirit. Thomas North, the English historian, translates Plutarch as writing "This was the first occasion. . . that made Caesar to love her. But afterwards, when he saw her sweet conversation and pleasant entertainment, he fell then in further liking with her". This was gently put.

Caesar then called Ptolemy back from Pelusium. He took longer to come than Cleopatra, but eventually all three were installed in parts of the splendid royal palace on the shores of the Mediterranean at Alexandria. This might suggest an uneasy trio; but as the world knows, things were not uneasy between Caesar and Cleopatra! The Roman, more than twice her age (Pl. IX) must have admired the young Queen's outstanding intellect, and her courage, befitting a descendant of Alexander the Great. His own strength of character, intelligence and determination must have struck a chord of joy in her, surrounded as she was by weakness and disloyalty.

Plutarch has not included Latin in the languages learnt by Cleopatra, but he took for granted that with her intelligence, her visits to Rome and her two Roman lovers it could be assumed that she understood the language. Although Caesar would not have spoken Egyptian, the educated Roman would have understood Greek, which was another tie between them. Plutarch emphasises that Cleopatra's beauty was not such that it assailed all who saw it; but her immense personality affected everyone who met her: the irresistible charm of her presence, he writes, the attractiveness of her person and her talk, which expressed a peculiar force of character and thought in every word and action, held all her listeners spellbound. "She had a wonderful voice"[3] writes one scholar; "it was a delight merely to hear the sound of her voice"[4] translates another; while a third adds: "like an instrument of many strings she could pass from one language to another".[5]

When some two weeks later the boy Ptolemy arrived at the palace, he may have been surprised to find his half-sister installed there, and certainly appalled to find that she and Caesar were in great accord. Doubtless palace gossip would soon have dismayed him further, when it reached his ears that they were lovers.

In Caesar's Report of this time, he notes that Pothinus resented him bringing Ptolemy to the palace, and that Pothinus brought some of Ptolemy's army from Pelusium, putting them in charge of Achillas, the murderer of Pompey. At this Caesar put his forces, although relatively small, to arms within the town, and he urged the young Ptolemy to send envoys of peace to Achillas. He did. And they were murdered. Caesar, in his wisdom, then took control of Ptolemy in the palace, to prevent the people beginning to think there would be armed warfare between them: in fact, there were already skirmishes between Achillas's forces and Caesar's men who were guarding the palace. Caesar, although with Cleopatra at night, which the writer does not mention in his report as Caesar already had a wife in Rome, joined his forces by day. They loved and trusted him greatly and he had full control over them. Then came battles by land and sea, but he out-manoeuvred Achillas by placing some of his Roman soldiers by the lighthouse, the 'Pharos', which was to become, like the pyramids, one of the 'wonders of the world'.

Meanwhile Arsinoe, Cleopatra's half-sister, who had also been sheltering and mischief-making in the palace, slipped out and joined Achillas. Some Alexandrians, who were delighted by Arsinoe's defiance of Caesar and Cleopatra, named *her* Queen of Egypt, which extended the basis of the war in Alexandria. Arsinoe had a eunuch adviser named Ganymedes, and soon rivalry

Plate IX. Portrait head of Julius Caesar

arose between him and Achillas, who was working with Pothinus and Ptolemy. Caesar discovered secret messages being sent to Achillas and had Pothinus put to death, possibly both for his own safety and that of Cleopatra. Having increased his army on the island of Pharos, Caesar then attempted to capture the causeway to it from the mainland. Caesar's own Reports are now continued by another writer. The Alexandrians came up behind Caesar's troops on the causeway, and confusion ensued. Caesar, remaining with his men, had to make for his ship. He was followed by the enemy who started boarding it, so he was forced to jump overboard. Although he was heavily armoured, shot at from all sides and submerged several times, he nevertheless managed to keep one arm aloft to save the papers he was carrying, as he swam to his ships further out in the harbour. Cleopatra might well have been able to see his leap for safety from one of the outlying buildings in the palace grounds, and would have feared for Caesar's life. It must have been a terrible moment for her, both personally and in the cause of her future. Caesar's own ship, which he had abandoned, sank with the invaders on board, but the set-back stiffened the resolve of Caesar's Roman legionaries, whose keenness to fight had to be restrained by him.

Eventually the Alexandrians sent to Caesar, asking him to release the young Ptolemy to join his friends. Although against the advice of his officers, Caesar agreed to release Ptolemy advising him to keep good faith with Rome. Ptolemy, perhaps as a devious gesture, burst into tears at leaving Caesar, but immediately he was free, waged war on him. We might guess the army officers would have said, "you see we were right"; but were they? The inexperienced boy King was pitted against the hard-headed intelligence of Caesar. At Pelusium, the eastern coastal garrison of Ptolemy, Mithradates, a great friend of Caesar's, was landing troops he had gathered in Syria. Ptolemy set out for his garrison with his large forces behind him. Caesar with his small force sailed there by sea. After several battles, Caesar pressed on to the King's camp and coming upon an unguarded rear position, shattered it. The King fled, and was taken aboard a ship which capsized; and he was drowned. When Caesar returned to Alexandria, the people capitulated, and he was received as a victor, having conquered the Greek city of Alexandria and Egypt at one time. He gave the people assurances that their freedom would be secure, and he kept his promise. His own heavily outnumbered forces were jubilant, and there can be no doubt whatever that Cleopatra, now possibly carrying Caesar's child, was overjoyed with relief. The writer who continued Caesar's memoires, narrates the latter event in a low key, merely stating that Cleopatra had remained loyal and stayed with Caesar's forces! Instead of annexing Egypt to Rome, which was what the Alexandrians had feared, he set Cleopatra back on her throne with her younger half-brother, Ptolemy XIV. The boy was only about 12 years old, but under the terms of Auletes's Will, he was destined to succeed his brother in the event of his brother's death. Caesar gave them Cyprus, which was a strategic gain for Egypt. He collected his debts; and King Cleopatra's head was once again represented, alone, on the coinage.

In the spring of 47 B.C., before leaving Egypt to continue his campaigns of conquest, Caesar went on a boat trip up the Nile with Cleopatra. How modern it sounds, a trip up the Nile. But it must have meant a flotilla of boats in their case. Their own boat, from comparative examples, must have been a floating palace. It was made from the cedars of Lebanon and Cyprus with a mixture of Egyptian and Greek decoration and furnished in the utmost luxury and comfort; sumptuous in the extreme. Probably this boat of Cleopatra's did not equal the magnificence of the one in which she was later rowed to meet Mark Antony at Tarsus, but the two journeys displayed a similarity in the close public association of the rulers of Egypt and Rome. Both Caesar and Antony had a wife in Rome, but their connection with Cleopatra - and Egypt - was stressed by their adoption of Egyptian customs and later, even their association with Egyptian gods.

Knowing as Caesar did about the decree denying the Upper Egyptians their share of the crop in a year of bad harvest, which had been associated with Ptolemy and Cleopatra's name, his shrewdness would have recognised the wisdom of such a journey. Now she was not only secure on the throne again, but she could be seen by these loyal subjects in the south as supported by Rome, in the person of Caesar himself. Time was to reveal her popularity there as although there had been risings in Egypt for nearly 150 years under the previous Ptolemies, there were none in her reign, until the people offered to rise up to support her against Rome. If Caesar did not promote this journey, he would certainly have seconded the idea. A medal of the time shows him adorned not only by a laurel wreath, in Roman style, but also a wide floral garland as worn by Egyptian men and women at banquets and entertainments. And in the great Luxor Temple, he is shown offering incense and a libation to the 'Great God Amen' who stands in an ithyphallic (creative) position before him.

All that was the diplomatic side of this journey. But for the lovers, the river provided a perfect setting, as romantic as even Cleopatra could contrive. Still only 23 years old, in love, restored as a king to her throne, she must have glowed with happiness and perhaps with that special radiance that some healthy young women have when carrying a child. Draped as she would have been in diaphanous robes of transparent linen with wraps of gleaming, soft silk from China, and groomed to perfection by her handmaidens, Caesar could also have enjoyed her educated and witty mind as the lazy days slid by. Welcomed by the people as they passed riverside villages and towns, seeing the desert colours, the grazing cattle, and the crops in the cultivated fields, and watching the women swaying gracefully with their water-carriers on their heads - as they do today and did in biblical days on their way to and from the wells - must have been as interesting as it was beautiful to the visitor from the West.

On their return to Alexandria Caesar prepared to leave, which was not surprising as he had been in Egypt for nearly a year. What fascination the country and its ruler had for the great Romans. He went to Syria and continued the promotion of the Roman state in the Near East. Meanwhile, Cleopatra busied herself with plans for a building on the sea-front at Alexandria to be called the 'Caesareum'. With a blend of Egyptian and Greek architectural features, it rose so high above the harbour that it became a guiding light for sailors, doubtless Cleopatra's idea of a monument worthy of the Caesars. A pair of obelisks were raised in front of it. One of these belonged to Thutmose III and is now in London, on the less sunny but historic Thames embankment and known rather ineptly as Cleopatra's needle. The Queen had a further memento of her lover, who had set her once more on her throne as a 'King' - his son. He was born soon after Caesar's departure and his origin was argued over by those politically affected throughout the Mediterranean world, and has been pondered over by historians ever since.

It was said that Caesar, although a lover of women, had only one other known child, his daughter Julia now in her 30s. Obviously that does not mean he had no other child, although 'unknown' would presumably have meant illegitimate. Caesar's nephew, Octavian, a man of towering, personal ambition who was bent on becoming Caesar's heir (and finally ended up as the Emperor Augustus), naturally denied that it was Caesar's son. Mark Antony, in the Roman Senate, bore witness that Caesar had acknowledged the boy as his son. Plutarch, almost within earshot of this politically important birth, is translated by North as writing that Caesar made Cleopatra his 'sister', who being great with child with him was shortly brought to bed of a son whom the Alexandrians named Caesarion, that is 'Little Caesar'. They were on the spot; privy to gossip, and with their fear of Rome would have been all too ready to make the point had there been any evidence that Caesar was not the father. It should be remembered that Caesar, by calling Cleopatra his 'sister' was aware that this was akin, in Egypt, to her being his royal wife. More than all this evidence there is one human factor not usually mentioned; had there been another man in Cleopatra's life at that time, gossip would have been rife. We can be pretty sure the news would have leaked out of the palace and reached us in some writings by now. In fact, during that year Cleopatra and Caesar lived as man and wife, it would seem to their mutual satisfaction. After Caesar's death, there is no evidence of any other lover in her life, apart from Mark Antony who eventually became her lover in every sense till the end of their lives. As summed up in the *Cambridge Ancient History* "she was by instinct, training, and pride-of-race a

Macedonian Princess". She was her own law, but intensely loyal to her two lover/husbands, and unlikely to have consorted with lesser men. In Cyprus, which had been Caesar's gift to Cleopatra and Ptolemy, a coin was struck showing Cleopatra suckling her baby. Here is the mother and son motif, reminiscent in Egypt of the Goddess Isis and her son Horus.

In the meantime, Caesar, after further victories, returned to Rome and despite some opposition was hailed as a dictator. He was a liberal and beneficent leader, but he knew he was not without enemies - absolute power is always close to the downfall of the great:

> "Let me have men about me that are fat;
>   Sleek-headed men and such as sleep o' nights:
>   Yond Cassius has a lean and hungry look;"[6]

and who better than Shakespeare could express the emotion of justifiable suspicion.

Later came the state visit of Cleopatra to Rome, with her co-ruler and young half-brother Ptolemy, and her (and Caesar's) baby son, accompanied by a small but impressive Court. It may have been her own, or Caesar's recognition, that besides his support of her as Egypt's King, in her father's Will, Auletes had actually asked that 'Rome' should support his wishes. With Caesar as dictator, there was no difficulty in re-establishing this important pact. The Egyptians arrived in great stateliness, and Caesar, returning the hospitality he had been given in Egypt, installed them in one of his own palaces. The indications are that, true to type, Cleopatra kept up a cultured and splendid little court, much favoured by influential, and no doubt ambitious Romans, while she was literally under the *aegis* of Caesar.

This period is scantily covered in the histories because of uncertainties and the destruction of many original sources. But we have some knowledge of one of Caesar's honours to her, and that a great one. After his triumphant return to Rome, he raised a new building, calling it the *Forum Julium*. It was walled, and in the centre of a colonnade, was a temple to *Venus Genetrix* who was regarded as the mother of the Roman people and protectress of the *House of Julian*. In this temple, he took the unprecedented step of placing a gilded statue of Cleopatra, a foreign ruler, and mother of his son, although he was married to a Roman woman, Calpurnia. In Rome, unlike Egypt where statues of Ptolemaic rulers were placed in temples, this was a brave gesture of alliance. It could well have been imagined as an affront by those wanting to annex Egypt, who certainly did not want to glorify, or even partly deify, its glamorous ruler. But Rome was to benefit from the specialists at Cleopatra's Court, and from Egypt's advanced civilization. The re-arrangement of the Calendar, eventually

117

to 365 days in a year, with an extra day in every fourth (leap) year, was introduced under the guidance of an Egyptian at her Court. Although not favoured at first, it was eventually adopted by Rome and, as the Julian Calendar is the basis of our own calendar today. Egypt's knowledge, and control of its life-blood, the Nile, and the irrigation from it, prompted ideas for using water supplies, including the draining of marshes and re-channelling of water into canals. Also Caesar, having seen the unique comprehensiveness of the Great Library at Alexandria, began to extend the Roman library system. He would, no doubt, have done more had his days been longer: but they were numbered!

He continued his conquests abroad, ignoring signs of bad health, but this may have led him to make his personal Will in 45 B.C. It astonished the world, when they eventually knew its contents. After his death, it was wrested from the vestal virgins with whom it had been lodged. To the shock and chagrin of many, he stipulated that at his death, his great-nephew, Octavian, should be known as his adopted son. There could be no mention legally of the illegitimate Caesarion, son of a foreigner, succeeding him, of which Cleopatra must have been aware. On the other hand, Mark Antony, the victorious cavalry officer and favourite of Caesar's must have been appalled. Despite Antony's bravery and gallantry, however, Caesar must have recognised that in the far less attractive and less lovable personality of his sister Julia's grandson, Octavian, there was a will-power that Antony lacked. He was ruthless and remorseless in his treatment of anyone in his way, which enabled him as the heir of 'Caesar' to become the Emperor Augustus of all the Roman Empire, which he helped to build. In spite of growing physical ailments, Caesar was planning a huge military exercise on the scale of Alexander the Great's, to regain Parthia in the east, where Crassus had been killed. But he set his sights too high and his power was too great for the liking of the senators. The 'Ides of March', 44 B.C. was the last dramatic moment in the history concerning Caesar. He was viciously attacked in the Senate, and, as we all know from Shakespeare and other accounts, stabbed and torn to death by over fifty of his senators. Savaged by his murderers, he fell dead at the feet of the statue of Pompey-the-Great, whom he had overcome on his rise to dictatorship. Of Cleopatra's reactions we can only guess: horror, disbelief - and then grief, in the knowledge that she had lost her lover and greatest friend - personal and political.

There is little recorded of her at this time, and we have to turn to Michael Grant in his book *Cleopatra* to gather the threads together. There are also some contemporary letters of Cicero's who hated Cleopatra's power (in fact did not much like women at all). Additionally there was also a personal enmity between him and Antony.

With a sorrowing heart and with her experience of political unrest, Cleopatra did the wisest thing and departed with her Court for home, in the knowledge that Caesarion was not in a position to benefit from Caesar's death. Caesar's great-nephew, and named heir, Octavian, returned from abroad, now calling himself 'Caesar'. Cleopatra realised that this was a direct threat to the life of her son, Caesar's own son. She reached Egypt in the summer of that year with her half-brother, Ptolemy XIV. He died in the autumn, aged 15. Historians are wont to suspect treachery on her part, and some hundred and more years later, rumours were recorded that she had him poisoned. There is no proof that she did; he could well have died a natural death in those climes, just indeed as Ptolemy XIII had died in war. But his death enabled the co-option of her baby son to be Ptolemy XV and to share her throne. She must have been desperate to secure his future, against the grossly ambitious Octavian (now alias Caesar), whom she knew would have had his eye on Egypt and not want Julius Caesar's son in his way. Again how right she was. It is possible she viewed her co-option of another male Ptolemy on to the throne with her - (although a very small one as yet) - as a continuation of her father's wishes. She adopted the title of *Thea Philopator* (Goddess who loves her father), giving her son that of *Theas Philopator Philometor* (God who loves his father and his mother), his father being recognised in Egypt as Julius Caesar. She perpetuated these symbols in the temples of her loyal people in Upper Egypt, having herself, and her son, carved in large scenes on the south rear wall of the Temple of Hathor at Denderah. They named him 'Ptolemy Caesar', son of Julius Caesar and Cleopatra, in the presence of the gods of Denderah, with Hathor the Goddess of love, in the centre.

At Hermonthis, further up-river beyond Thebes, where she had taken part as a young girl-monarch in the river procession of the Apis Bull, the buildings have been destroyed for the stone, but there was a birth temple, celebrating the birth of the infant Horus and Caesarion. Horus, it will be remembered, was the son of the Goddess Isis, with whom Cleopatra closely associated herself. How different from Amarna and the worship of the Aten was the Egypt of Cleopatra's day which had reverted to all the ancient gods and goddesses.

The death of Caesar was inevitably a watershed in Roman history. However disappointed Antony became when he found that he in no way featured in Caesar's Will, we have, as created by Shakespeare, his wonderful funeral speech to his "Friends, Romans, Countrymen" with his ironic naming of the murderers as "honourable men"! But even more telling is his spontaneous outcry in the Capitol at the time just after the murder:

> "O mighty Caesar! dost thou lie so low?
> Are all thy conquests, glories, triumphs, spoils,
> Shrunk to this little measure? Fare thee well.
> I know not, gentlemen, what you intend,

Who else must be let blood, who else is rank.
If I myself, there is no hour so fit
As Caesar's death hour."[7]

In this lament Shakespeare ennobled both men.

Brutus and Cassius, the two leaders in the murder, fled abroad and began to assemble troops in the East, fearing war against them by Octavian and Antony. Cassius went to Syria, where Dolabella, a loyal friend of Caesar's clashed with him. Both sent to Cleopatra for help. Naturally she sent some of the Roman legionaries but only to Dolabella, not to Caesar's murderer. But Dolabella was defeated. This weakened Cleopatra's military strength, and left Cassius with greedy eyes on Egypt. Her mischief-making, half-sister, Arsinoe joined in sympathy with the Governor of Cyprus, who supported Cassius. This fraught situation was overcome by Brutus calling Cassius back to Asia Minor. In Rome, a threatening coalition of Antony, with Octavian, and a weaker link, one Lepidus, became the ruling triumvirate. They virtually ruled the Roman world. Cleopatra again refused to help Cassius, on the plea of a low Nile and bad harvest. Although she feared Octavian, she decided to take the short view. She set sail in her flagship out of the harbour of Alexandria, leading her fleet on Caesar's side, en route to support Antony and Octavian. But a bad storm arose and shattered her boats, and she was forced to return home. There were, however, two decisive battles in Greece, at Philippi, in her own antecedants' territory of Macedonia, where Antony, leading the Caesar faction, was completely victorious. Both Brutus and Cassius died, on their own initiative, as Romans. Octavian and Antony then agreed to divide the Roman world: Octavian took the West; Antony took the East, giving Lepidus Africa. Here began the first line of relevant histories written about the following events in the next twelve years.

III   Cleopatra and Mark Antony

Shakespeare was but a teenage boy when the famous translator, Thomas North, decided to translate into his vivid English *The Life of Mark Antony* (Marcus Antonius), which had been written so long ago in Greek by Plutarch. North, afterwards Sir Thomas when knighted by Queen Elizabeth I, based his text largely on the previous translation made by the scholarly Jacques Amyot. It proved a fateful coincidence of timing - if there are coincidences - for North's translation fell into the hands of Shakespeare, and on it the poet based his incomparable play *Antony and Cleopatra*. Thus the play is so much more than the superb poetry in it, being as it is so truly based on history; and at the same time it is so much more than the history itself, as written by this inspired playwright, with his great insight into the characters of the people caught up in the dramatic events of the period.

Dr. Scott Kilvert believes that the "Life" of Mark Antony is in many ways the most ambitious and brilliantly executed of all Plutarch's biographies. This he attributes to Cleopatra and the history of her life. "Nowhere else" he writes "do we find a woman of the stature of Cleopatra, and the sweep of the narrative touches the very bounds of the Roman Empire itself, from the Alpine snows to the deserts of Parthia" (Persia) "and from the plains of Philippi to the palaces of Alexandria".[8] Plutarch lived from the mid-40s A.D., with one foot in the pre-Christian world and the other, in his maturity, in the years of early Christianity. He had contemporary records to use, most lost to our own historians; and he was able to hear from his grandfather, stories told to *him* by a doctor who had been in Alexandria at the time of Cleopatra. This emphasises the vast difference between this *historical* period, and the archaeological period which requires the piecing together of what happened centuries earlier, from remains such as fragmentary stone inscriptions and carvings and the chance findings of what people wore, ate and used.

Plutarch discerned Antony's charisma and the love and loyalty he inspired in his troops, without seeing his great weaknesses as part of the whole man. So nearly a contemporary of this period, Plutarch would have known of Rome's fears and doubts, and the hatred built up against Cleopatra, although he gives full accounts of her irresistible charm, her power, her glowing personality and brilliant intellect. Plutarch records that Antony had the generosity and honesty for which his father was known, and the distinguished bearing of his nobly born mother Julia, of the Caesar family. The boy gave early promise of zest, but in later youth his excesses, partly engendered by his exuberant energy, became habitual and his character was weakened by them. He was self-indulgent, and became unduly licentious even for a dashing young man. He drank excessively; was an indiscriminate lover of women, and ran up debts he had no way of meeting. Although he fell into bad company in Rome where politics raged and corruption was not unknown, he did not really falter in his allegiance to Caesar, who loved the youth and tried to steady him.

Eventually Antony went to Greece where he developed a love of Greek culture and things Grecian which remained with him all his life and must have been a lasting source of pleasure between him and Cleopatra. He threw himself into military training and athletics for which he was physically endowed, but despite this more spartan period of his life he still tended towards dissipation. We know that previously, in his late 20s, he had already distinguished himself as a brilliant cavalry commander when in 55 B.C. he came to the support of Cleopatra's father, Auletes. After the battle he spared disloyal troops from Auletes's vengeance, and buried his opponent Prince Archelaus of Asia Minor, whom he had once visited, with honour. This is the essential core of the best attributes in Antony's character: bravery in battle; magnanimity in victory.

Plutarch describes him at this time as having a noble presence. He was thickly bearded and seemed in his dress to adopt a Herculean pose (Hercules being regarded as an ancestor). He drank and dined with his soldiers; was unusually liberal with them, and they adored him. North translates that he enjoyed hearing their love stories. Shakespeare notes Cleopatra's appreciation of his looks as she remarks to her lady-in-waiting Charmian -

> "Look prithee Charmian,
> How this Herculean Roman does become
> The carriage of his chafe"[9]

- i.e. his spirited bearing. It must have been a blow to Antony to find himself entirely omitted from Julius Caesar's Will. He was recognisably senior to Octavian, the new so-called Caesar, in every way; more experienced, and certainly a more distinguished soldier. It was Antony who fought the battle at Philippi against Caesar's murderers, when Octavian, some twenty years younger, fell ill and left the field. It is significant that as one of the three rulers of the Roman Empire, as it was then, Antony chose the Eastern section. He knew that Caesar, before he died, was planning to renew the campaign to annex Parthia. This large territory stretching inland over what was once Persia (now Iran) from the Caspian Sea to the Persian Gulf, with its capital Seleucia on the Tigris river, would have been a big prize for Rome, although oil was not then the world's incentive. The Roman ruler Crassus had been defeated by the Parthians and it would have hugely extended Rome's prestige, to acquire this territory. At this time, Antony's provinces already included Greece, and Asia Minor (Turkey) with its developed centres at Ephesus and Pergamum; and southwards, Syria too, which was west of Parthia, was under Roman influence.

Plate X. *Antony meets Cleopatra* by Tiepolo

IV   Antony Sails Eastwards

Antony sailed first for his beloved Greece, then to Asia Minor where he gathered support, and amassed considerable riches. But with a campaign against Parthia in mind, Egypt was clearly needed for its strategic position as the gateway to the East, for financial support and for food from its plentiful grain crops. No one could ignore its monarch Cleopatra, her Ptolemaic wealth and that of Egypt itself. If Antony had talked to her even when she was a teenager, he would inevitably have been impressed with her startling intelligence and charm. He sent an invitation for her to meet him at Tarsus, in the south-east corner of Asia Minor. She delayed suitably as a monarch to a co-ruler, but eventually set out northwards to cross the eastern end of the Mediterranean, passing Cyprus en route to Tarsus near the coast of the then Cilicia. Here again we have the history of her glamour and another example of her incomparable style. The preparations she had been making for her visit turned it into the most artistically described visit by one ruler to another in the whole of history. Prose-writer Plutarch must have heard of her journey up the river Cydnus described in such glowing terms, that in his writing of its beauty, his phrases and imagery as transmitted by North, literally inspired Shakespeare. Nothing could exceed their accounts as a tribute to her journey and arrival. Although Shakespeare blended the ideas as one would expect of a poet, Plutarch endowed the woman with her full force. No longer the girl who, wrapped in a carpet had been brought to Caesar in her own Palace, but a woman of grace and experience in the prime of her life, who came displaying sumptuous splendours. The poop of her barge was of gold, wrote Plutarch:

Plate XI. Mark Antony on a coin

125

" the sails of purple, and the oars of silver, which kept
stroke in rowing after the sound of the music of flutes,
howboys, citherns, viols, and such other instruments as
they played upon in the barge. And now for the person
of herself: she was laid under a pavilion of cloth of
gold of tissue, apparelled and attired like the goddess
Venus commonly drawn in picture, and hard by her, on
either hand of her, pretty fair boys apparelled as
painters do set forth god Cupid, with little fans in
their hands, with the which they fanned wind upon her.
Her ladies and gentlewomen also, the fairest of them
were apparelled like the nymphs Nereides (which are
the mermaids of the waters) and like the Graces, some
steering the helm, others tending the tackle and ropes
of the barge, out of the which there came a wonderful
passing sweet savour of perfumes, that perfumed the
wharf's side, pestered with innumerable multitudes of
people. Some of them followed the barge all alongst
the river's side; others also ran out of the city to
see her coming in; so that in the end there ran such
multitudes of people one after another to see her that
Antonius was left post-alone in the market-place in
his imperial seat to give audience. And there went a
rumour in the people's mouths that the goddess Venus
was come to play with the god Bacchus, for the general
good of all Asia."

" When Cleopatra landed, Antonius sent to invite her to
supper to him. But she sent him word again, he should
do better rather to come and sup with her. Antonius
therefore, to show himself courteous unto her at her
arrival, was contented to obey her, and went to supper
to her; where he found such passing sumptuous fare,
that no tongue can express it. But, amongst all other
things, he most wondered at the infinite number of
lights and torches hanged on the top of the house,
giving light in every place, so artificially set and
ordered by devices, some round, some square, that it
was the rarest thing to behold that eye could discern
or that ever books could mention. The next night,
Antonius feasting her contended to pass her in magnificence and fineness; but she overcame him in both." [10]

It is fascinating to see what poetry Shakespeare made of this description:

> "The barge she sat in, like a burnish'd throne,
>   Burn'd on the water: the poop was beaten gold;
>   Purple the sails, and so perfumed that
>   The winds were love-sick with them; the oars were silver,
>   Which to the tune of flutes kept stroke, and made
>   The water which they beat to follow faster,
>   As amorous of their strokes. For her own person,
>   It beggar'd all description: she did lie
>   In her pavilion - cloth-of-gold of tissue -
>   O'er picturing that Venus where we see
>   The fancy outwork nature: on each side her
>   Stood pretty dimpled boys, like smiling Cupids,
>   With divers colour'd fans, whose wind did seem
>   To glow the delicate cheeks which they did cool,
>   And what they undid did." . . . .

> Upon her landing, Antony sent to her,
> Invited her to supper: she replied,
> It should be better he became her guest;
> Which she entreated: our courteous Antony,
> Whom ne'er the word of 'No' woman heard speak,
> Being barber'd ten times o'er, goes to the feast,
> And for his ordinary pays his heart
> For what his eyes eat only."[1]

For the first time Antony was met by a woman's "No"; met and for once overcome: for once - and it can be said forever. He became entirely enraptured; infatuated would not be too strong a word for his life-long attachment to her. (Pl. X) Shakespeare saw the couple as immortal lovers, caught in the tangle of world history, helpless against the rising tide of Roman ambition -

> "The nobleness of life
>   to do thus, when such a mutual pair
>   and such a twain can do't,"[2]

The dramatic couple quickly became linked in people's minds with the gods: Antony with Bacchus (Dionysus) whom the Greeks associated with Osiris; and Cleopatra with Venus (Aphrodite) and long associated with Isis, so the transition to a husband/wife relationship was easily established *in the East.*

Despite the banquets and entertainments at Tarsus, however, the meeting was not all dalliance and dancing. Antony was anxious to be reassured, as indeed Cleopatra could and did reassure him, that she had been ready to fight with him in retaliation of Caesar's murder, and that she was actually sailing to his assistance at Philippi when a storm struck her ships and she was forced to lead them back to Egypt. She, for her part, was able to point out to Antony that although he had been welcomed in splendour at Ephesus, there was an anti-Roman faction there, led by her jealous half-sister Arsinoe. She was still sheltering there after her previous attempt to depose her father when he had gone to Rome. Additionally she had sided with the Governor of Cyprus against those who fought for the memory of Caesar at Philippi. Antony had her taken from Ephesus and executed. This, as with other political murders ordered by Antony, were laid by some at Cleopatra's door. But Antony had been ruthless in the civil murders he had previously ordered in Rome, and would not have been tolerant of forces which could rise against Rome. The Governor of Cyprus had not only been disloyal to his sovereign Cleopatra by supporting Cassius and Arsinoe, who was aspiring to be queen: he had also supported the murderers of Caesar and was therefore clearly against the three rulers of the Roman world: Antony, Octavian Caesar, and Lepidus, and for that reason alone, Antony would have had him put to death. It is easy for most countries in the Twentieth century to understand how some rulers can use their power to 'liquidate' those they regard as enemies!

Antony needed Egypt: and it was to Egypt he returned for the winter of 41-40 B.C., or it could be put another way: he returned to Egypt with Cleopatra. He came to Alexandria where he had previously gained favour for his magnanimity in victory, and, with great tact, he came as a Roman visitor to the Court of Cleopatra, rather than as a Roman ruler. The first winter they shared in Egypt set the pattern for the lively entertainments, even revelry which occurred whenever these two were together. Plutarch records his grandfather's account (told by a physician in Alexandria at the time) that eight boars were roasted for a dinner of only twelve people - but roasted one after another so that many suppers were cooked to enable *one* to be at the perfect stage for eating, whenever Antony arrived after extended activities - including drinking.

From the coins of this time it appears that the ruling Queen/Goddess was adopting a more sophisticated, curled style of hair dressing, with increased adornment of her robes. This was a departure from her plainer Greek styles in favour of pearl trimmings. Pearls had to be brought from the seas of India and the Red Sea; they were costly but they were fashionable in Rome. The strong face, however, full of vitality, with the tip of the nose downturned like her father's, is still shown on the coins.

Her surroundings continued to be lavish; and of a magnificence unknown in Rome. Buildings had marble walls with rafters supporting the ceilings masked in thick gold; floors were of alabaster (plentiful in Egypt); doors of ebony and ivory, which continued the decorations of centuries past with gifts from the south. Other descriptions include "gem-ridden couches", presumably with drapes thrown across them, otherwise very uncomfortable which does not seem likely. The jasper and other stone used for cups and goblets was in the Egyptian tradition; as was the gold and silver tableware. The Romans accused Cleopatra of being a harlot, because of the descriptions of the riches of the East, ignoring the traditions of the past from which they sprang.

Although Antony was known as a great lover of women, as noted before there is no evidence that Cleopatra had any other lovers but him and Julius Caesar. Few accounts are left of the intellectual life at Court, but with Cleopatra's learning and Antony's love of Greece, and Alexandria the absolute centre of learning in the ancient world, there was probably a more cultured background there than in many capitals of the time. She inherited the encyclopaedic sources of knowledge that were lodged in the Museum and the famous Library of Alexandria, which had been set up and financed by earlier Ptolemies and was maintained by her. These two buildings, where research was habitual, were in the precincts of her palace and she would have found immense fascination in conversing with the international scholars working in them. Her lively intellect and her education would have enabled her to appreciate their findings and in turn, would have sparked off their minds and stimulated them. It has been written that she deeply enjoyed the pleasures to be found in books. Her wit, the quality of her mind, with its concern for deeper studies and the joyous sights and colours with which she surrounded herself must have quickened the senses of those around her and been a large part of her magnetic personality, which her enemies narrowed down to sexual charm alone.

Cleopatra constantly accompanied Antony. She shared his pleasures in gaming, hunting, fishing and even the jollities of singing in the streets under the stars blazing in the indigo night sky. Nevertheless she encouraged his resolve to continue his unfinished campaign to annex Parthia, which was beginning to attack Rome's eastern provinces. She could see how this would strengthen his standing in the Roman trio of rulers. He sailed off eventually to join his troops in Syria, some of whom had defaulted to the Parthians during the unduly long period of inactivity. Then he received dispatches saying that his wife Fulvia and his brother had unsuccessfully campaigned against Octavian, and had been forced to flee from Italy. He was thus in difficulty both to the East and the West, and circumstances separated him from Cleopatra for three years. Some might have wondered whether this would have driven a wedge between them and ended their love affair. Indeed in Rome it was hoped that it would. But as a French courtesan once shrewdly remarked, love more often dies from too much than too little.

Antony left his conquest of the East and turned to Rome. He blamed Fulvia, who was now ill, for her senseless rising and made off for Italy, where after some skirmishing, he managed to come to an agreement with Octavian. In 40 B.C. the pact for the rule of the Roman Empire by the triumvir was extended, with Octavian still controlling the Western half, Lepidus in charge of Africa, and Antony keeping his hold on the East. In the meantime Fulvia died of her illness.

Rome was anxious and bitter about Antony's alliance with Egypt and her regnant Queen, and plans were laid to keep him at home. Octavian had a beautiful sister Octavia whom he greatly loved and admired and who had recently been widowed. Fulvia was dead. Antony did not lay claim to Cleopatra as his *wife* although he did not deny that he 'kept' her, a rather strange statement of their alliance considering her wealth. However, everybody worked to bring about a marriage between Antony and the noble Octavia and although her widowhood was legally too recent to allow another marriage, this legal hitch was overcome in Rome and Antony was married to her. They went to Greece where Octavia had their first daughter, Antonia. Octavia was never to bear him a son, whereas Cleopatra was to bear him two. But it was Octavia who brought up his heir Antyllus, his eldest son by Fulvia. He spent three winters with Octavia, relinquishing his campaign in Parthia to which he sent Ventidius to do battle. While in Athens, Antony received news that Ventidius twice overcame the Parthians in battle, but then returned to Athens for fear his success might offend Antony. It seems a pity he did not follow up his victorious conquests, being the only man to overcome the Parthians, and with hindsight, one can only assume that Antony would have been glad to have been rid of the task.

However, these victories increased Antony's reputation, which may have brought about the quarrel with Octavian whom it is written, Antony had offended. So Antony sailed back to Italy, to Tarentum, on the inner coast of the 'heel' of the country in the south. Octavia went with him. She was carrying his third child by this time, and she acted as peace-maker between Antony and her brother. Antony feasted Octavian who promised him troops to use against the Parthians (a promise never to be fulfilled), while Antony promised to give Octavian ships to help his continuing conquests. Despite Octavia's pleas to accompany Antony he sailed off to the East again without her. But as she had six children already to care for, including her own, Antony's and their own daughters, and she was again pregnant, it was easy for him in the circumstances to send her home and not let her accompany him to war (and incidentally Cleopatra).

As he approached the sights, sounds and perfumes of the East his longing for Cleopatra grew stronger and he sent for her to come to Antioch in North Syria, where he 'married' her. They spent the winter of 37-36 B.C. there together, although they must both have realised that the conquest of Parthia by Antony was a task inherited from Julius Caesar and would have been a bigger triumph than anything Octavian could hope for. It was vital both territorially for Rome and for Antony's prestige. He gave Cleopatra gifts of land in Phoenicia and Syria; Cyprus (again), part of Cilicia south of Asia Minor, the region of Judea and the coastal strip of Arabia down to the Red Sea. The Romans, of course, resented this rebuilding of the old Ptolemaic Empire for Egypt, and more still his enhancement of Cleopatra's power. They were not appeased by the fact that she had borne him twins who were acknowledged by him. His son he named *Alexander* Helios (the sun), a combination of her famous ancestor and the emblem of the sun which was on his coins; and his daughter *Cleopatra* Selene (the moon). Plutarch makes the point that Antony who liked to think of himself as a descendant of Hercules was not ashamed at begetting numerous families.

Plate XII. Cleopatra in her thirties

V   The Parthian Campaign

Cleopatra returned to Egypt and Antony journeyed to Armenia (north of Parthia) where the King of that country supplemented his Roman army, bringing the number of troops to over 50,000. Plutarch writes that it was Antony's overwhelming desire to stay with Cleopatra and to return to her as soon as possible that made him go to war too early in the season, instead of wintering in Armenia so as to give his men time to recover from their arduous journey. Then he could have invaded in the spring in a surprise attack.

But he hurried his army, and perhaps that was why he allowed a catastrophic mistake to occur from which it never recovered. He overlooked the supervision of the invaluable siege equipment - the huge battering rams to break down walls, and battery engines for storming fortresses. This equipment was carried in 300 carts which were left behind the troops! In the heights of Asia where there were no trees of the strength or height to replace the battering rams, he began besieging the greatest city of Media (which bordered the Caspian Sea near Parthia). But without his irreplaceable 'siege train' he could not breach the walls. While his army were engaged in an attempt to mount them, the King of the city discovered Antony had left his equipment behind and sent an army to encircle it. They killed 10,000 of Antony's men, took many others prisoner, and burnt the battery engines.

The Romans were devasted by this loss at the beginning of their campaign and the Armenian King withdrew the men he had lent Antony, in despair of his success. Greatly encouraged, the Parthians advanced and attacked Antony's camp, but Antony counter-attacked by a great charge and sent them flying. Here we see once again the brave cavalry officer, although afterwards the Romans found they had lost more men in the fray than they had killed and captured.

In all this, Antony's battle-bravery was remarkable, but he lacked the powers of a military strategist and administrator, and the strong will of Julius Caesar who was able to oversee the affairs of every part of his army, without leaving anything essential undone (or behind him!). Possibly Antony's mental powers never reached the ability of ordering and controlling Rome's largest army of the time, and now, in his late forties, after a licentious life, he had lost the power of great concentration. Dr. Tarn, in the *Cambridge Ancient History*, probably put his finger on the basic trouble by defining Antony as "born to be second, not first; as he had been with Caesar, so he was to be with Cleopatra and Octavian". His warm-hearted, ardent nature could not command the cool judgement and resolve of conquerors like Hannibal, Alexander and Julius Caesar.

The rest of the campaign is largely a story of death, disease and famine amongst his gallant and loyal troops. Most impressive, writes Plutarch, was "the respect, the obedience, and the goodwill they showed towards their general"... "they preferred Antony's good opinion to their own lives and safety". His troops could have done no more. In misery and remorse he visited the sick and dying. An indecisive victory was then accomplished by him, but the troops increasingly suffered from famine or were poisoned by the roots and herbs they ate and the bad water they drank. They died from hunger and thirst, dropsy and dysentery. Eventually they reached Armenia again having suffered, according to Plutarch, the devastating loss of 20,000 foot soldiers, and 4,000 horsemen. Their passing victory over the Parthians was not followed up. Antony sent for the King of Armenia, who had withdrawn his troops, and then kept him prisoner.

From there he pressed on to the Mediterranean, sending for Cleopatra to come to him on the coast, losing 8,000 more men on the snowy march. Near Sidon, in 35 B.C., he waited for Cleopatra, whose arrival was later than he expected, slowed down, no doubt, by gathering reinforcements for him. Plutarch gives a merciless account of his frenzied drinking, and his constant rushing to the coast to see if her ships were in sight. There was no doubt of his need for Cleopatra as a woman; but there was also his need for the supplies she was bringing him. Octavian had not weakened his forces by remaining faithful to his promises of troops for Antony. When Cleopatra eventually arrived she bore clothing for the soldiers, money to pay them (although some said this was his, given by him, but in her name) and of course in the Asian lands he had given her, she had the great cedars of Lebanon which he needed for shipbuilding, at which the Egyptians were greatly skilled.

Despite her devotion to Antony, Cleopatra must have realised by now, with dismay, just how far short he fell as a military strategist. In her heart she may have been building him up to the stature of her ancestor Alexander or to Julius Caesar, who allowed nothing to stand in the way of their military ambitions and she must have begun to see in Octavian the strength of purpose discerned by his uncle. She and Antony had been working towards their dream of a partnership in ruling the kingdoms of the East, which could then be handed on to her children, always supposing they could overcome Octavian's growing ambition to conquer the world. It was this partnership of Cleopatra's strength behind Antony, that Rome was to fear. If her confidence in him was shaken, her love for him was not; it was not in her indomitable spirit to give way.

Octavia sent offers to Antony to bring him troops, pack-animals and money; he wrote to Athens to send the supplies but did not ask her to come herself. Antony probably guessed Octavian was denying him his due, although Octavia, trying to bind Antony to her brother, still offered to help him. Cleopatra saw the strong position that Octavia held, being linked as she was to Octavian, and is said to have feigned ill health out of love for Antony. But she may well have been laid low by his divided position and his shilly-shallying. This was evident by his postponing until the summer what promised to be a fortuitous moment to attack Parthia, which had just fallen out with the Medes. But instead of attacking he returned to Alexandria.

Octavian flaunted this in Rome with various other of Antony's failures, turning erstwhile friends against Antony, and reviling him for his desertion of his wife. It looks too as though he also stirred up trouble for Antony in the Near East. Antony tried to patch up his previous quarrel with the King of Armenia by offering his and Cleopatra's small son Alexander for betrothal to the small daughter of the King, whom he invited to visit Alexandria. But the King refused and Antony launched an offensive against Armenia in 34 B.C. Cleopatra, possibly to give him moral support, accompanied him on his journey East all the way to the Euphrates, where she left him. He marched to the capital of Armenia to make terms, which the Armenians refused. Then Antony finally arrested the King and took him and his family and much treasure back to Alexandria. There seems little evidence of a real campaign at this stage, which was in any case only a stepping stone to Parthia. Antony is said to have left his best general and troops in Armenia, and to have given some of the Armenian territory to the Medes, with the offer of his son (rejected by the King of Armenia) to the King of Media for his small daughter. Then he returned to Alexandria.

Dr. Michael Grant gives an account of Cleopatra's journey from the Euphrates.[13] It would seem she made triumphant progress: a slow *tour de force* with her regal procession and entourage. She had the bravery, charisma, and glamorous presence that never failed to win admiration. Her presence always created a ceremonial occasion. She first visited a city in Syria; then journeyed further along the Orontes river to the lands of a native chieftain, and her command of languages must have been a tremendous surprise and honour to those she met. Then she went to Damascus where her kingship was welcomed as a sign of support against marauding invaders. Next, on entering Judea, she encountered Herod whom she had once tried to displace as a leader and who was therefore in no way pleased to receive her. But he had to, for the sake of

Antony's friendship and support. The strength of the unalterable tie between Antony and Cleopatra seems to have been fully recognised in the East. Historians after the event have written that Herod was madly jealous of Cleopatra's power and wanted to murder her, which may well have been true. Other historians, writing over a century after the event, accepted the gossip that she had tried to seduce Herod. Nothing, it would seem, could have been less likely. She hated him; but apart from that, her innate dignity, her status as a Greek princess, King of Egypt and now of its Empire, and her true love for Antony puts this theory far out of court. Another report suggests that whatever sinister plans Herod may have harboured, it appears in fact that he plied her with gifts and escorted her some of the way back to Egypt, which seems the more politic behaviour for him to have adopted at this time.

The build-up of stories that Cleopatra was a whore is understandable. Her attractions were such that with a lift of a finger she could have had any lover she wanted. But history reports only the two great Romans, Caesar and Antony, as her lovers. Her power over these Roman leaders led to envy in Asia, and fury in Rome. And, however tactful she was, her pride must have caused bitterness and spite amongst rejected admirers, presumably numerous, although no other names remain linked with hers.[14] In Rome, Octavian was stirring up more hatred against her because of Antony's neglect of his noble wife. This led to the legends of the "poisonous charms of Cleopatra"; this "seductive", "oriental", "luxury loving" woman. The stories that remain in some history books and in some people's minds today that she was a shallow-minded siren, beautiful (which she was not), and constantly indulging in promiscuous sexual pleasures are unsubstantiated, and all ignore her active rule of her country, her wisdom, and her culture. From a purely practical point of view, her undoubted love for Antony, her ambitions for Egypt, and her Macedonian protectiveness towards her children, would have prevented her being unfaithful to Antony which would have weakened her hold over him, and undermined his trust in her. At the end of their lives, when he thought she had betrayed him, he lost his sanity and endeavoured to take his own life. Perhaps Cleopatra viewed the resentment against her too lightly because she knew how strong the bond was between her and Antony, and their shared hope of a ruling 'partnership' in the East: but Octavian wanted to rule the world. There seems little she could have done except give up Antony and send him home, sealing the fate of Egypt and leaving her children in the power of Rome. But the bond and the hope was too strong for that.

VI   The Tension Snaps

What Antony organised on his return to Alexandria shows exactly how deeply Cleopatra must have hoped to restore Egypt's Ptolemaic Empire. Antony entered Alexandria this time as a conqueror. There he staged a theatrical display, unique in spectacular and political significance, for all to see. It was called the 'Donations' and was of a size and splendour more usually attributed to Cleopatra. After all, he had her 'tools'; the skill of the Egyptians and the earlier Ptolemies' gold and silver. The reason for it being called the 'Donations' of Alexandria gets easier to understand as the pageant proceeds. In the athletic arena, in front of multitudinous crowds, Antony and Cleopatra sat on golden thrones raised on a silver dais. How these must have glowed and sparkled in the sun. He declared that she had been the wife of Julius Caesar and that Caesarion was Caesar's son. (This fact of course threatened Octavian, but when he remonstrated, Antony claimed that Cleopatra was his wife now, and pointed to Octavian's love affairs).

During the display, Cleopatra was robed as Isis and Antony portrayed in statues as Osiris/Dionysus, so that the 'marriage' of this god and goddess was again proclaimed. There were smaller thrones below them for Julius Caesar's son Caesarion and their own three children. He declared Cleopatra to be the "Queen of Kings", and Caesarion, "King of Kings", and joint monarch with her of Egypt and Cyprus. Alexander, the twin boy, now six years old, was dressed as a Parthian king with a peacock feather in his turban. He received the Kingdom of Armenia and the overlordship of Parthia and Media, although Antony had not yet conquered Parthia. His twin sister Selene became Queen of Cyrenaica and Libya in North Africa. Little Ptolemy Philadelphus, now two, wore Macedonian dress and was made overlord of Client Kings West of the Euphrates as far as the Hellespont (Dardanelles).

Antony had a commemorative coin struck featuring his head on one side with the words "Armenia Conquered", while on the other side Cleopatra was designated "Queen of Kings and of her sons who are Kings". No wonder Rome gasped. She was head of the whole hierarchy. Antony himself was not King of

Kings; he was greater; it would not seem his desire to become King of the Eastern territories of Rome. If he was aiming at ruling the whole of the Roman Empire, Cleopatra would be beside him in the East, and she would be a Roman Empress. Dr. Tarn criticizes the statement that Cleopatra drove Antony to ruin as unimpressive: "he need not have been driven",[15] he wrote. But the underlying threat to Rome, if such it was, became more explicit.

In Rome people were tired of the civil wars. In 36 B.C. Octavian announced that the wars were over, resulting in a united Italy. Octavian continued to fight abroad, where his soldiers and his brilliant Admiral Agrippa reaped success. At home he beautified Rome. Naturally Octavian reported Antony's 'Donations' to the Roman Senate. It has been said that Octavian cared little that Antony gave Roman territories to client kings, which was apparently a well-known habit at the time; and that he ignored Cleopatra as a 'Queen of Kings'; but he did object strongly to the consequence regarding Antony's position because he, while remaining a ruler in Rome, was also a divine monarch in Asia - beside Cleopatra. This brought the hitherto manageable tensions to snapping point and a war for the world between Antony and Octavian became inevitable. Cleopatra's paramount concern was the fate of Egypt and her children. She recognised Antony's position and Octavian's ruthless obsession to rule the world; she had seen much of what sort of crimes conquerors perpetrated. But she expressed no personal fear; she did not sail off down the Red Sea with her children leaving Egypt without a king, open to attack from the west. She looked both ways. She faced the dilemma and she prepared to throw in her all. Antony was warned by her enemies to kill Cleopatra and annex Egypt himself. If these supporters of Antony recognised the bond between him and Cleopatra, they ignored it. Antony knew some of his officers and men would fight with him in any situation; but some of the officers were demanding the condition, that Cleopatra should go back to Egypt.

Antony's response was to give works of art and the library at Pergamum to the library in Alexandria, allowing a suspicion to grow that he might make his capital there.

Together, Antony and Cleopatra mobilised a great fleet for which Cleopatra provided half the 'transport of ships' and many rowers, as well as food for the army and navy from Egypt. Plutarch points out, in answer to pleas that she should be returned to Egypt, that she was largely feeding and paying the forces, and that in wisdom and judgement she was second to none. Thus Cleopatra's and Antony's forces were joined and sailed to the Greek island of Samos where a round of festivities began. They visited Athens where Cleopatra was greatly honoured. Antony sent word to Rome to expel his wife Octavia from his house, where she was looking after her own children; his by Fulvia (except his eldest son Antyllus who was now with him) and their own daughters. People pitied her; and those who knew Cleopatra's personality pitied Antony. He was inescapably divided.

Octavian was surprised to find Antony's fleet prepared, but instead of using it to attack then, Antony 'stood by' in Greece and gave Octavian time to levy heavy taxes on the Romans to equip his own forces. He literally sat waiting for Octavian to get ready and continue his barrage of hate. Eventually Octavian gathered his smaller fleet in the harbours at the heel of Italy, and in 31 B.C. sailed, unmolested, across the Adriatic. Here in transit Antony might well have dealt him a smashing blow; his and Cleopatra's forces were the larger and it seems extraordinary that Cleopatra could not have overcome his lethargy and urged him to attack the approaching fleet while it was crossing the sea. Apparently there was controversy between them, Antony favouring war by land (the cavalry officer); Cleopatra a sea battle. She was right *at this moment of events,* and had she taken the lead the result may well have been very different. But this would have drawn Egypt into the battle as a nation, and bloodshed and massacre would have followed in her own country.

As it was, Egypt itself was never violently overwhelmed, for later when Octavian was finally at its gates and the country wanted to rise for Cleopatra, she forbade it, wanting to prevent useless suffering for her people. The Roman fleets (with hers supporting Antony) met at Actium on the promontory on the east coast of Greece just north of the isthmus of Corinth. It was surely one of the most curious battles ever fought. Instead of the strategies of a war, it would, seem that human frailties ruled. Plutarch wrote of this battle, and since then there have been many accounts. Shakespeare makes the faithful Enobarbus say to Cleopatra:

> "He is already
> Traduced for levity, and t'is said in Rome
> That Plotinus, an eunuch, and your maids
> Manage this war."[16]

A few lines later in the play Antony enters and asks how Octavian crossed the sea so quickly to which she replies, leaving little doubt of her feelings:

> "Celerity is never more admir'd
> Than by the negligent."[17]

The fight[18] was delayed until the enemy was fully protected in harbour: too late. Antony's fleet lay idly in harbour at Actium. Meanwhile Octavian's Admiral Agrippa had led an attack around the Peloponnese and cut off Antony's grain ships supplying him from Egypt. Antony disembarked and camped with his army opposite Octavian's troops hoping to cut off their supply of water which was at risk.

Then comes one of the most surprising and saddening events. Antony's attack was defeated by the failure of his cavalry. This must have been the 'last straw'; his cavalry-prowess gone. Desertions from his army began. Antony, instead of besieging Octavian was now besieged himself and withdrew to the ships. His troops and crews were attacked by disease, said to be from wintering on low ground, but doubtless worsened by despair. Desertions increased and Antony knew that deserters would become informers for Octavian, but like so many leaders, he believed, as he had reason to do from the past, that his men would follow him to the last. He made great plans to take advantage of a prevailing wind from the north-west, which usually arose after midday. He knew Octavian's fleet would be waiting outside the harbour and planned to take advantage of the wind to drive it southwards.

He made a second plan, known only to himself, Cleopatra and one other, for which he took sails on board. It was clearly a plan to operate after a defeat, should they break away and sail to Egypt leaving Antony's troops to follow overland. Possibly his order to ship the sails (for this plan) indicated flight to his followers who were fighting for a Roman, but not anticipating a fight for Egypt against Rome. When the wind slewed south, not only Antony raced to take advantage of it but as might have been expected, Agrippa did too.

The fight began - and then the squadrons at Antony's centre and left returned to harbour; the inner squadrons on his right surrendered and he was left with nothing but his personal squadron on his right, which engaged in battle, and Cleopatra's which was by then, isolated. He signalled her to carry out plan two, for flight. She hoisted sail and stood by to the south, possibly waiting to see if she could still help him or whether she should return to protect Egypt. Antony's flagship was grappled and he transferred to the first ship of the line and with some forty of his fleet, followed Cleopatra. He boarded her flagship and sat at the prow with his head in his hands - a broken man from that hour.

But Cleopatra remained steadfast. She saw the battle was over and believed they lived to fight again. She sailed into the harbour at Alexandria with head erect and ships garlanded for victory. Every plan now depended on Antony's co-operation. She tried to stir him from his dejected inactivity, but he made no attempt to collect the troops to defend and hold the enormously strong line of the Nile which had so often saved Egypt from invasion. Cleopatra, with her unfailing courage had therefore to decide whether she would defend Egypt by herself against Octavian (Caesar) whose advance on it now was inevitable. She was again a client ruler of Rome. That she would lose her throne on Octavian's successful invasion, Cleopatra knew full well: she would be too strong a ruler to leave on a throne. But if she fought to hold her throne, her country and her children might fall with her, and there was always the possibility that Octavian might let her crown pass to her son as a subject ruler to Rome. She made her decision. In her wisdom, she must have known there was no other practicable course to take. It was at this moment that her country wanted to rise and fight behind her leadership, but she forbade it, to prevent her people suffering. Nevertheless, at her death, the Upper Egyptians rose against the Romans.

Octavian came on his mission of conquest from Syria in the summer of 30 B.C. He pitched his camp outside Alexandria and Antony made a last valiant attack on him and with a success that must have raised his spirits, drove Caesar's horsemen back: the last charge of the cavalry officer. Shakespeare gives Cleopatra the lifting, loyal words:

> "It is my birthday
> I had thought to have it poor; but since my lord
> Is Antony again, I will be Cleopatra."[19]

She was 40 years old. She put the Ptolemaic riches: gold, silver, emeralds, pearls, ebony and ivory into the ground floor of her tomb, a huge mausoleum she had built. Antony sent a challenge to Octavian to fight him man to man. Octavian replied that there were many other ways Antony might find to die. He probably reckoned that the world would not accuse him of killing Antony and Cleopatra if they chose to die by their own hands! Legends arose round Alexandria from that night that weird noises were heard presaging the death of a leader - as Shakespeare wrote it:

> "Tis the God Hercules whom Antony loved
> Now leaves him."[20]

The next morning he went up to the hills by the city and watching his galleys rowing out to sea thought they were going to fight the enemy. What abandonment of mind this shows - his fleet operating without his leadership, or even his orders. It was being rowed to Octavian's men, but not to engage in battle: they saluted them and were saluted in return. Then the two sides joined forces and rowed together towards Alexandria harbour. Antony ran back crazed and crying that Cleopatra had betrayed him, and she, afraid of his madness, fled to her tomb and locked and barred the doors, going up to the first floor. Perhaps she planned to fire the treasure and die in the flames. She sent word to Antony that she was dead. At last she realised his complete loss of strength. He withdrew, but instead of falling on his sword as noble Romans did, he asked his follower Eros to kill him. Eros drew his sword, but fell on it himself.

"Thrice nobler than myself!
Thou teachest me, O valiant Eros, what
I should, and thou couldst not. My Queen and Eros
Have by their brave instructions got upon me
A nobleness in record . . . Come then -"[21]

and he fell upon his sword, but did not kill himself. In the meantime Cleopatra sent for him to come to her tomb, and when he heard she was alive he begged for his body to be taken to her. Her two ladies, Iras and Charmian, helped her to haul his helpless, bleeding body up to her on the first floor of her mausoleum, and were deeply distressed to see her straining every muscle in her neck and back to bring him up. Cleopatra took him in her arms. Antony's last words to her, with her reply, forecast the future:

"I am dying Egypt, dying . . . one word sweet Queen:
Of Caesar seek your honour and your safety."[22]

and Cleopatra's reply shows Shakespeare's understanding:

"They do not go together."

He died in her arms and she tore her hair and her breast in her grief. That day Octavian entered Alexandria without resistance. He sent Proculeus to take Cleopatra alive, as he was afraid she would destroy the treasure. She spoke to him through a grating and sent a request that her children might succeed her. The next day Octavian sent Romans to seize her. She tried to stab herself but was disarmed, and searched in case she had poison concealed in her clothes. She was then taken to him, in her own palace. Her treasure was safe for him at last; he could pay his army and his Roman debts with her wealth.

He now allowed her to return, giving orders to *prevent* her killing herself, perhaps envisaging having her dragged through the streets of Rome in chains. Then he went to see her, as she was overcome with grief and feverish from her self-inflicted wounds. She stood before him so he could see her mutilated condition and yet, writes Plutarch: "the force of her beauty was not altogether defaced": surely it was the force of her unquenchable spirit which shone through. Octavian made her lie down. Her treasurer gave details of her fortune, but when he contradicted her she rose and took him by the hair and boxed him - to Caesar's amusement. She asked that some things from her possessions should be given to some of her friends, as a means of reassuring Caesar that she did not mean to burn her treasure or take her life; and so he left her. One of his court who befriended her told her that Octavian intended to send her away soon, with her children. He would not have wanted her in Egypt with a loyal following. She asked permission to visit Antony's grave, where she was carried, and fell upon it speaking aloud, as though to him, said many things as Plutarch reports, including:

> "Whilst we lived together, nothing could sever our
> companies. But now at our death I fear me they will
> make us change our countries. For as thou being a
> Roman hast been buried in Egypt, even so wretched
> creature I, an Egyptian, shall be buried in Italy . . .
> If therefore the gods where thou are now have any
> power and authority, sith our gods have forsaken us,
> suffer not thy true friend and lover to be carried
> away alive, that in me they triumph of thee. But
> receive me with thee, and let me be buried in one
> self tomb with thee. For though my griefs and
> miseries be infinite, yet none hath grieved me more,
> nor that I could less bear without, than this small
> time which I have been driven to live alone without
> thee."[23]

There we have as near as it is possible, Cleopatra's answer to those who said she loved Antony not - save for her own ambition. She be-flowered the tomb and returned to hers and then dressed herself as though to dine. While she was seated at table came the countryman to her, with the well-known basket of figs in which lay the asp she had asked for, whose bite had the power to kill quickly. Barring all the doors, the asp was released to give its fatal bite:

> "Come thou mortal wretch,
> With thy sharp teeth this knot intrinsicate
> Of life at once untie: poor venomous fool,
> Be angry and dispatch."[24]

Octavian sent messengers running to her, but they were too late. She had died with the dignity with which she had lived, on a gold bed in her regal robes. One of her women was dead at her feet; the other, Charmian, the guard found was:

> "Trimming up the diadem
> On her dead mistress; tremblingly she stood
> And on a sudden dropp'd."[24]

"Is it well done?" asked the messenger and Charmian just managed to reply:

"It is well done and fitting for a Princess
Descended of so many royal Kings."[24]

Even Octavian, when he heard, is dignified by Shakespeare as saying:

"Bravest at the last
She levell'd at our purposes, and being royal
Took her own way."[24]

Octavian killed the young Caesarion, her son by Julius Caesar; and Antony's son and heir Antyllus. The ambitious conqueror, who became the Emperor Augustus, could not allow young regal heirs to continue to breathe.

It has been written, and it is a partially fitting epitaph for Cleopatra the Great, that "Rome, who had never condescended to fear any nation or people, did in her time fear two human beings; one was Hannibal, and the other was a woman."[25]

FOOTNOTES

1 William Shakespeare, *Antony and Cleopatra* 2 *ibid.*
3 W. W. Tarn, *Cambridge Ancient History*, 1934
4 Michael Grant, *Cleopatra*, 1974
5 Ian Scott-Kilvert (trans.), *Plutarch, Makers of Rome*, 1977
6 William Shakespeare, *Julius Caesar* 7 *ibid.*
8 Ian Scott-Kilvert (trans.), *Plutarch, Makers of Rome*, 1977
9 William Shakespeare, *Antony and Cleopatra*
10 T. J. B. Spencer (ed.), *Shakespeare's Plutarch*, 1968
11 William Shakespeare, *Antony and Cleopatra* 12 *ibid.*
13 Michael Grant, *Cleopatra*, 1974
14 Professor Grant writes of the Ptolemaic Queens that they were "habitually chaste (more chaste than the Roman Empresses of the future)" and they "would have found it hard to acquire lovers worthy of their grandeur". From *Alexander to Cleopatra*, 1977
15 W. W. Tarn, *Cambridge Ancient History*, 1934
16 William Shakespeare, *Antony and Cleopatra* 17 *ibid.*
18 W. W. Tarn, *Cambridge Ancient History*, 1934
19 William Shakespeare, *Antony and Cleopatra* 20 *ibid.* 21 *ibid.* 22 *ibid.*
23 T. J. B. Spencer (ed.), *Shakespeare's Plutarch*, 1968
24 William Shakespeare, *Antony and Cleopatra*
25 W. W. Tarn, *Cambridge Ancient History*, 1934

Bibliography

LIST A - on the general history of Ancient Egypt (mostly published before attention was drawn to Nefertiti's regality).

An Introduction to Ancient Egypt: (a compendium of the general history with articles on the writing, religion, arts and crafts, and lists of principal pharaohs and Roman emperors with dates). T. G. H. James (British Museum).
Ancient Centres of Egyptian Civilisation: Egyptian Education Bureau, London.
The Archaeology of Ancient Egypt, T. G. H. James (Bodley Head).
The Art and Architecture of Ancient Egypt, Stevenson Smith (Penguin Books, London). (See Queen Hetepheres, Chapter V, plate 30).
Egypt, Lange and Hirmer (Phaidon (London), Oxford). (Rameses II with small figure of Queen, plate 241).
Egypt in Colour, M. S. Drower (Thames & Hudson, London).
The Sculpture of Ancient Egypt, C. Desroches-Noblecourt (Olbourne Press, London).
Egyptian Art, J. R. Harris (Hamlyn Group, Middx., England).
The Scepter of Egypt, W. Hayes (Metropolitan Museum, New York).
The Legacy of Ancient Egypt, edited by J. R. Harris (Oxford University Press).
Treasures of Tutankhamen, I. E. S. Edwards (British Museum).
The Remarkable Women of Ancient Egypt, Barbara Lesko (Scribe Publications (Box 4 705), Berkeley, California 94704, U.S.A.).
A Thousand Miles up the Nile, Amelia Edwards (reprinted Century Press, London, 1982).

LIST B - relating to Part I.

The books for Part I are largely on excavations and other basic sources of information about Amarna. Some subjects have been indicated with their relevant books to help readers trace specific interests.

Specialist books are not readily available from bookshops or general libraries. They can of course be found in University and Museum libraries, not easily accessible, and in the invaluable library of the Egypt Exploration Society, London, of which membership is not confined to Egyptologists. This Society has been responsible for fundamental publications on Amarna and to prevent repetition, the abbreviation 'E.E.S. London' has been used. Aris and Phillips, Warminster, Wiltshire is abbreviated to 'A. & P. Warminster'.

Tell el Amarna, Sir Flinders Petrie (reprinted A. & P. Warminster, 1974).
The Rock Tombs of El Amarna, Vols. 1-6. N. de Garis Davies, 1903-1908 (E.E.S. London). These contain reproductions of the scenes in the rock tombs of the nobles which are essential for a visual idea of Amarna life.
Amarna, City of Akhenaten and Nefertiti : Nefertiti as Pharaoh, J. Samson (A. & P., 1978).

The Royal Tomb at El-'Amarna, Vol. I. G. T. Martin (E.E.S. London). This contains reproductions of the objects which have been saved. Volume II is in press (E.E.S.).

City of Akhenaten, Vols. I-III, particularly III by John Pendlebury and others, and I (South Palace) by Woolley and others. (E.E.S. London).

The Tomb of the Vizier Ramose. N. Garis Davies (E.E.S. London).

Nofretete (Nefertiti), R. Anthes, Egyptian Museum, West Berlin.

The Akhenaten Temple Project, Vol. 1. R. Smith, D. Redford and others. (A. & P. Warminster, 1976). This publishes some of the building blocks recovered from the destroyed Aten temple at Karnak, Thebes.

Akhenaten, D. B. Redford (Princeton University Press).

Scarabs and Cylinders with Names, Sir Flinders Petrie, University College London. For 'news scarabs' of Amenophis III see plate 21.

Akhenaten, C. Aldred (Thames & Hudson). See Karnak statues, plates 2-4.

New Kingdom Art in Ancient Egypt, C. Aldred (Academy Editions, London). For carving of Nefertiti as elderly monarch see plates 124-25.

Amarna Reliefs from Hermopolis in American Collections, J. Cooney (Brooklyn Museum, U.S.A.).

Journal of Egyptian Archaeology (J.E.A.), (E.E.S. London). For the palace mural of royal family see vol. 7.

Mural Paintings of El 'Armaneh, N. de Garis Davies, Nina de Garis Davies, E. Frankfort, S. R. K. Glanville (E.E.S. London). See North Palace chapter III and plates II-XII.

Secret of the Gold Coffin, G. Perepelkin, Moscow.

Das Ende der Amarnazeit, R. Krauss (Hildesheim).

Some *Articles* in specialist journals on Nefertiti's regality:

Göttinger Miszellen 4 (1973), J. R. Harris.

Chronique d'Egypte XLVIII, J. Samson, 96 (1973).

ACTA Orientalia (Copenhagen University), J. R. Harris, 35 (1973), 36 (1974).

Chronique d'Egypte, J. R. Harris, 97 (1974). On the identity of Kiya.

Göttinger Miszellen, J. Samson, 32 (1979), 53 (1981), 57 (1982), 63 (1983).

LIST C - relating to Part II.

This historical period is largely documented in translations and books easily accessible to the interested reader.

Shakespeare's Plutarch, edited by T. J. B. Spencer (Penguin Shakespeare Library).

Plutarch, Makers of Rome, translated by Ian Scott-Kilvert (Penguin Classics).

Caesar, The Civil War, Translated by Jane Mitchell (Penguin Classics).

Plutarch, The Fall of the Roman Republic, translated Rex Warner (Penguin Classics).

Cleopatra, Michael Grant (Panther Books).

Cambridge Ancient History, Vol. X. (Cambridge University Press), Chapter III.

Plutarch - Age of Alexander (Penguin Classics). Gives the full life of Cleopatra's conquering forbear.

Ancient History Atlas (from 1700 B.C.), Michael Grant (Weidenfeld & Nicolson). Revised edition is inestimably useful.

Index

Concordance of U.C. objects and page number

Concordance of University College (UC) objects mentioned with short description.